Table Of Contents

FLASH 5

in easy steps

NICK VANDOME

COMPUTER
STEP

In easy steps is an imprint of Computer Step
Southfield Road . Southam
Warwickshire CV47 OFB . England

http://www.ineasysteps.com

049370
28-2-02

Notice of Liability
Every effort has been made to ensure that this book contains accurate
and current information. However, Computer Step and the author shall
not be liable for any loss or damage suffered by readers as a result of
any information contained herein.

Trademarks
Flash™ is a trademark of Macromedia Inc. All other trademarks are
acknowledged as belonging to their respective companies.

£9.99

Printed and bound in the United Kingdom

ISBN 1-84078-126-2

7 Bitmaps and sound 99

8 Frames and layers 111

9 Animation 127

Interactivity   147

Testing and publishing   171

Index   187

Introducing Flash

This chapter gives an overview of the functions of Flash 5 and the uses to which it can be put. It shows how to obtain and install the program and gives details of the Flash environment when it is first opened.

Covers

Chapter One

Life before Flash

If there is one constant about the Internet and the World Wide Web it is the speed at which they develop. As recently as the beginning of the 1990s Web users were excited about the possibility of viewing coloured static text and a few small, equally static, images. However, since then Web site designers and developers have harnessed advances in technology with a desire to create increasingly complicated multimedia output. This includes animated images, animated text, page transitions, sound and video.

Bandwidth is a term used to describe the amount of digital data that can be sent down a telephone cable and the speed at which it is sent. A higher bandwidth means that more information can be sent down a cable, and so reach the user's computer more quickly. Since multimedia files can be a lot larger than their static counterparts, increased bandwidth is vital for them to download quickly enough to keep the user's attention.

Increased bandwidth for the Internet is an area that telecommunications companies are constantly working on improving.

Initially even the most basic multimedia effects on the Web came at a price: downloading time. In a lot of cases the infrastructure for downloading multimedia pages was just not up to the task, with the result that these types of pages took a long time to appear on the user's computer. The result of this was a lot of annoyed users and a lot of sites that were left unvisited because they took too long to download.

But as with everything on the Web, the technology has not been slow to catch up and, due to increased bandwidth for downloading and more advanced browsers for viewing, it is now possible to enjoy truly exceptional multimedia experiences on the Web, without having to wait an eternity for the files to download.

In addition to increased bandwidth, software programs for creating multimedia sites have become increasingly powerful and this is where Flash comes in. Flash is an animation program that can produce high quality multimedia files. In addition to this it uses a number of techniques to ensure that the final product is as streamlined as possible, thus creating files that can be downloaded reasonably quickly. Three of the most important aspects of Flash in this respect are:

- Vector-based graphics

- Streaming

- Compression

How Flash works

Vector-based graphics

Traditionally, images on the Web have been bitmaps i.e. images that are made up of pixels, or tiny coloured dots. In general, the more pixels in an image then the better the quality. However, each pixel adds to the file size of the image and so you have to walk a fine line between quality and file size. Also, when a bitmap image is resized it can deteriorate in quality: if it is enlarged, then each individual pixel has to cover a larger area. This can result in the edges looking jaggy or ragged. The three types of bitmap images that are used on the Web are GIFs (Graphical Interchange Format), JPEGs (Joint Photographic Experts Group) and PNGs (Portable Network Group).

GIFs are created with 256 colours so they are generally used for graphics that do not have an enormous range of colour depth. JPEGs use 16 million colours and are more commonly used for photographic images. PNGs are not yet as popular as GIFs or JPEGs but they can produce good quality images with small file sizes.

Since one of the main functions of Flash is creating drawing objects, it is vital that it can do this in an efficient and high quality way. It achieves this by using a vector-based system for producing graphics, rather than a pixel-based one. A vector-based system is one where objects, lines and fills are created using mathematical equations. The computer then interprets this equation and displays the corresponding image on the screen. This has two considerable advantages:

Drawing programs (such as Macromedia Freehand and Adobe Illustrator) use vector-based systems for creating graphics.

- Since vector-based images do not consist of any actual pixels, they are usually a lot smaller in file size than their bitmap counterparts. Even very complicated vector-based images create comparatively small files, regardless of how large or small a size they are displayed at

- Vector-based images lose very little image quality when they are resized, since they are still based on the same mathematical equation. So, if a bitmap circle is increased in size, its edges may begin to look ragged. However, a vector-based circle would appear smooth regardless of how it was resized. This combination of small file size and high quality makes vector-based graphics ideal for Web pages

A Flash file is known as a movie.

Streaming is a bit like reading a book by having each page handed to you as you need it: you know it is all there, but you can only read one part at a time so seeing the whole thing at once would be pointless.

Another important way in which Flash controls the overall file size of a movie is through the use of Symbols and Instances. This allows for copies of an original image to be used numerous times without adding to the size of the movie. This is covered in greater detail in Chapter Six.

Streaming

The end product created by Flash (called a Flash movie) can be either a few seconds long or several minutes. With the former, downloading time is not a big issue because the browser should be able to download all of the movie and play it almost simultaneously. However, with the latter the situation is not so straightforward. Even with all of the tricks it has up its sleeve, Flash would be hard pushed to produce a movie that would play for several minutes and yet be compact enough to download in a few seconds.

Flash overcomes this problem with a technique called streaming. This feeds information to the browser as it needs it to play the movie, without having to wait for the whole thing to be downloaded to get started. So initially Flash will feed enough of the movie for the browser to start playing it and the user will see this on their monitor. As the movie begins to play, Flash continues to feed information to the browser, enabling it to play the next part of the movie. This is streaming in action and it means that even the longest Flash movie can be viewed without having to wait hours for it to begin after downloading.

Compression

Most images on the Web are compressed in one way or another. GIFs, JPEGs and PNGs all use various forms of compression to decrease their file size. In the majority of cases this has, at worst, only a minimal effect on the final image. One reason for this is that computer monitors can only display between 72–96 pixels per inch. This is known as the resolution and if an image has a higher resolution than this then it is creating an unnecessarily large file, with extra pixels that cannot be displayed.

Flash uses a variety of sophisticated compression techniques, for both images and sounds. The technical side of this is best left to the experts but there are some preference settings that can be used to determine various compression settings. These will be looked at in the relevant chapters.

The uses for Flash

If you are creating Web pages that include Flash movies it is important to include a plain HTML version of the document. This is because not all users will be able to, or want to, download the Flash Player that is needed to view Flash movies. So on the home page of a Web site there could be three links:

- *to the Flash version of the site*
- *to the HTML version, and;*
- *for downloading the Player*

Web authoring

Although Flash movies can be output through a variety of devices, their main function is in the production of Web pages. However, there is one important point that should be remembered in relation to this: Flash movies have to be incorporated into HTML documents to enable them to be displayed on the Web. This means you have to create the HTML pages for your site and then insert the relevant Flash movies. Luckily, Flash has a facility for producing HTML files that incorporate Flash movies and this is looked at in Chapter Eleven. The end result looks complicated, but Flash takes care of most of this behind the scenes.

Presentations

In addition to be being used on Web pages, Flash movies can also be used as a presentation tool. To do this, the Flash movie is played through a computer as a stand- alone application. This is known as creating a projector and this is a self-contained executable program that can play a movie regardless of whether the user has the Flash Player installed or not.

E-commerce

Flash contains a powerful programming language, called ActionScript, which is ideal for using on e-commerce sites that need a bit more than animations and simple interactive actions. In Flash 5, ActionScript has been enhanced so that the programming syntax is the same as for Javascript. Therefore anyone with a knowledge of Javascript will quickly feel at home with ActionScript. This can then be used to create complex online order forms and other elements that are integral to an e-commerce site. However, a good knowledge of programming is still needed to use this feature to its full potential.

Flash movies can also be exported into video formats such as QuickTime or a Windows .AVI movie.

What Flash can do

Both the animation functions and the interactivity ones in Flash can seem a little daunting at first and Flash is certainly more complex than a program such as a standard word processing package. However, if you work through the functions of Flash in a logical order, and do not expect too much too soon, then you will build up a good, solid foundation on which to base your Flash authoring activities. The aim of this book is to provide this foundation.

Animation

It is perfectly possible to produce Flash movies that contain nothing more than static text and images. However, if this is your aim you would be well advised to use an HTML program such as FrontPage or PageMill if you are creating Web pages and PowerPoint if you are creating presentations. One of Flash's main reasons for existing is its ability to animate both text and graphics. If you do not use this then you are overlooking at least 50% of the program's capabilities.

While Flash may not turn you into the next Walt Disney it does offer a considerable range of techniques for the budding animator:

* Text that fades in and out or moves across the screen

* Frame by frame animation, using either objects you have drawn yourself or items you import into Flash

* Tweened animation, a technique where you set the start and end point for an object and Flash automatically creates an animation between (hence the name) the two points. Tweened animations can be in the form of either motion or shape tweens

A shape tween animation, also known as morphing, changes one simple shape into another during the animation:

1 ꝣ 2

* Guided animation, where you create a path which the animated object can follow

Animation in Flash is dealt with in more detail in Chapter Nine.

Interactivity

Another key element of Flash is interactivity. This allows the user not only to view a Flash movie but also to interact with it. This makes users feel as if they are actually part of the movie they are viewing and that their actions affect what is happening on screen.

Interactivity in Flash is created by assigning certain values and properties to buttons and text boxes so that one action triggers another, predefined one. This opens up numerous possibilities for Flash movies:

Creating interactive elements in a Flash movie is one of the more complex areas of the program. It is important to feel comfortable with the rest of the program before you begin using interactive functions. See Chapter Ten for more information on interactivity.

Flash 5 has improved scripting facilities so it is much clearer to see which interactive actions are associated with a particular part of the overall movie.

- Buttons can have action commands assigned to them, to define what acts as a trigger. This can be when a button is pressed, when it is released, or when the mouse cursor passes over it

- Buttons can have actions that play sounds at certain points in the movie

- Buttons can be programmed to jump automatically to another part of the same movie

- Buttons can be programmed to open up other pages on the Web

- Buttons can be used to create a Menu bar

- Text boxes can be used to display a personalised message to the user when they insert an item of text, such as their name

- Text boxes can be used to collect information about the user. This is done with an interactive form and the data is then collected by the server that is hosting the page with the Flash movie on it (if the Flash movie is on a Web page)

Obtaining Flash and the Flash Player

There is virtually no difference between the PC format of Flash or the Mac one. Most of the screen views and menus are identical. Any differences will be noted as and when they occur.

Flash is produced by Macromedia and detailed information about the program can be found on their Web site at:

- http://www.macromedia.com/software/flash

This contains general information about the program, demos of how it works and links to sites that use Flash.

To download a 30-day trial version of the program, click here:
   This is a fully functioning version of the program that will stop working at the end of the trial period.

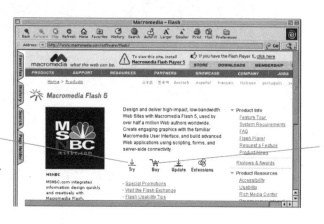

The Flash 5 home page on the Macromedia site. Click here to download the program

In addition to downloading Flash, you can also buy the program from computer shops and software retailers. The price is approximately £240 and this includes disks for the PC and the Mac formats.

The Flash Player

In order to view a Flash movie on the Web, the Flash Player has to be installed on the user's computer. This is a plug-in application that allows the user to see the Flash movie playing. The Player is installed automatically when you install the full authoring program of Flash. However, if you want to view Flash-enabled Web pages before you buy the program then you will have to download the Player. This can be done from the Flash Home Page at:

- http://www.macromedia.com/software/flashplayer/

If you do not have the Flash Player installed and try to view a Flash Web site, a message will appear, prompting you to download the Player.

As Flash becomes more popular on the Web, so more and more browsers have the Player pre-installed. It has been estimated that 96% of Web users can view Flash without having to download the Player. However, always include a link for downloading the Player, just to be on the safe side.

Installing Flash

Playback for Flash 5 via the Flash Player requires the following features:

- *Windows 95, 98, Me, NT, 2000 or later (Mac OS 8.1 or later for Macintosh users)*
- *Internet Explorer 3 or later*
- *Netscape Navigator 3 or later, or;*
- *A Java-enabled browser if you are using the Java Edition of the Player*

If you are using an older version of a browser the easiest option is to upgrade to the latest version. These are free and can be found at:

- *http://www.microsoft. com for Internet Explorer, and;*
- *http://www.netscape.com for Netscape Navigator/ Communicator*

If you are installing Flash by downloading it from the Macromedia Web site, or from a CD-ROM, the process is similar. When the program begins to run, the Flash 5 Installer icon will appear. Double-click on this to go to the Flash introduction window. Click OK and then follow the step-by-step instructions that take you through the installation process. Flash will set up folders on your hard drive for the program and, unless you have a good reason not to, it is best to install the program files here.

System requirements

The system requirements for Flash 5 have to take into consideration the authoring program and also the Flash Player for viewing the end results (see the tip).

Windows authoring

- 133 MHz Pentium processor
- Windows 95/98, NT4, 2000 or later
- 32 Mb of RAM
- 40 Mb of disk space (ROM)
- 256-colour monitor with minimum 800 x 600 resolution
- CD-ROM drive

Mac authoring

- Power Mac or iMac with OS 8.5 or later
- 32 Mb of RAM
- 40 Mb of available disk space (ROM)
- 256-colour monitor with minimum 800 x 600 resolution
- CD-ROM drive

The Flash environment

The following areas have been added or enhanced in Flash 5:

- *Improved timeline*
- *Standard Macromedia user interface*
- *Pen tool*
- *Shared Symbols Libraries*
- *Enhanced drawing tools*

Once Flash has been installed, it can be opened by double-clicking the Flash icon that the installation process should have placed on the Desktop (Windows) or in the Finder (Mac).

The first view

When Flash is first opened, a new, blank document will be displayed on screen. This is the Flash authoring environment and it contains the elements that are needed to create a Flash movie. At first sight, it can seen a bit overwhelming, but each item has an important part to play in the authoring process:

The Panels are another area that has been enhanced in Flash 5 and they will be looked at in relation to the relevant items as they occur throughout the book. The Panels can be accessed by selecting Window>Panels from the menu bar or from the Launcher at the bottom right corner of the program.

This is a feature that has been incorporated into several other Macromedia Web authoring products, such as Dreamweaver and Fireworks.

The Menu bar   The Standard Toolbar (Windows only)

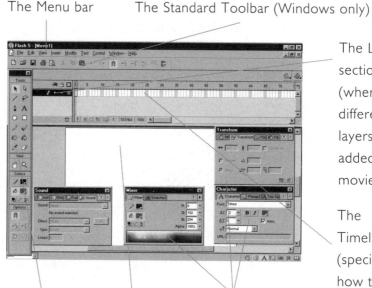

The Layers section (where different layers are added to a movie)

The Timeline (specifies how the movie is played and various actions)

The Drawing Toolbar (holds the drawing tools)

The Stage (the content for each movie is placed here)

The Panels. These display information about items within a Flash movie

The elements of the Flash authoring environment are looked at in greater detail in Chapter Two.

Getting started

This chapter looks at the elements that make up the Flash authoring environment. This includes the means for controlling the content of a movie, the area where movies are created, and the toolbars, menus and panels that are used during the editing process.

Covers

Chapter Two

Basic functions

New files

Open files

Opening and closing files

Flash movies are created in the Flash Editor section of the program and this is the environment that appears when Flash is launched. The Editor opens with a new, empty document called Movie1. All new movies that are created in the same editing session are called Movie... and numbered sequentially, until they are saved and given a unique name. To create a new Flash movie:

1 Select
File>New from
the Menu bar

2 The new movie is
opened and its
current name is
displayed here

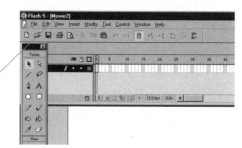

To open an existing Flash movie:

1 Select
File>Open
from the Menu
bar

2 Click on the file
you want to
open and select
Open

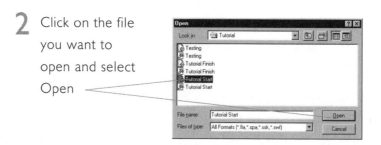

The Timeline

 If you want to create more space on the Stage for editing purposes, you can hide the Timeline. Select View from the Menu bar and click on Timeline so that there is no tick next to it. To make the Timeline reappear, reverse the process so the tick is showing.

The Timeline is the section of Flash that enables you to organise all of the elements that make up your movie and see what is placed at certain points throughout your publication. The Timeline organises items such as scenes, layers and frames and it is also used to create animated effects. Of all of the elements of Flash, the Timeline is probably the most important and also the most complicated for the novice as there is no equivalent in other software packages.

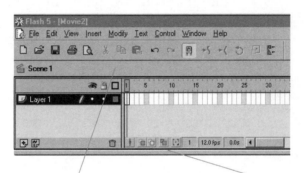

The Timeline contains several powerful organisational functions

Click and drag here to reposition the Timeline

Click and drag here to resize the Timeline

 Layers are a very versatile way to control content while you are editing Flash movies. They are discussed in greater detail in Chapter Eight.

Elements of the Timeline

Layers   Layer controls   Playhead   Frames   Frame rate

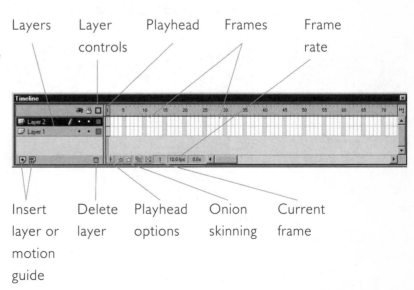

Insert layer or motion guide   Delete layer   Playhead options   Onion skinning   Current frame

The Stage

The Stage is the area where all of the content for a Flash movie is placed. This can be done by drawing objects directly onto the Stage, dragging them from the Flash Library or importing them from other applications. At any given frame in a Flash movie, the contents for that frame are displayed on the Stage. So the contents for frame 1 could look very different from the contents of frame 20 in a movie. The grey area around the Stage is known as the Work Area and this can be used to place animated objects that appear or disappear from the edge of the Stage. Only items that are visible within the Stage area will appear in the final movie.

The Flash Stage can be thought of in the same way as a theatre stage: anything that is placed there can be viewed by the audience.

Current scene

Click and drag the Playhead to move between the frames of a movie. The content for each frame that is covered by the Playhead will be displayed on the Stage

Edit scene

Edit symbols

To hide the Work Area, select View from the Menu bar and deselect the tick next to Work Area. To display it again, reverse the process.

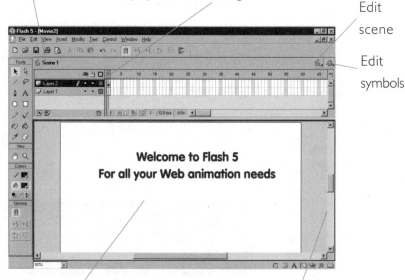

The Stage, displaying the content for the current frame (in this case frame 1)

The Work Area. Items placed here will not appear in the final movie but it can be a starting or ending point for items that move on or off the Stage

Movie Properties dialog box

There are a number of settings that can be applied to the Stage and these are accessed through the Movie Properties dialog box:

1 Select Modify>Movie from the Menu bar

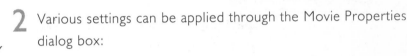

2 Various settings can be applied through the Movie Properties dialog box:

Frame rate

Stage dimensions

Background colour

Save new default

Ruler settings

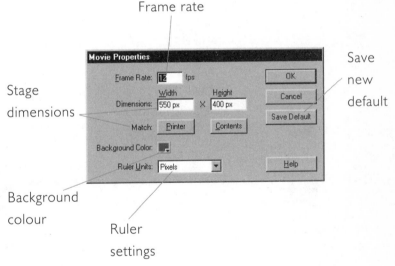

The settings in the Movie Properties dialog box affect a Flash movie as follows:

- *Frame Rate.* This is the speed, in frames per second, at which the movie is set to play. The default setting is 12 frames per second and this is regarded as a reliable standard setting for animations viewed on the Web

To set the
Stage size to
exactly fit the
content in a
specific movie,
select Match>Contents from
the Movie Properties dialog
box. Flash will then
automatically calculate the
dimensions required for the
Stage.

- *Stage Dimensions.* This specifies the size at which the Stage is displayed. Type values into the Dimensions boxes to make the Stage larger or smaller as required

- *Ruler settings.* This specifies the unit of measurement for all affected items on the Stage: rulers, grids and Stage dimensions. The choices are: inches, decimal inches, points, centimetres, millimetres and pixels

- *Background.* For these settings, see below

Setting the background colour

The default background colour on the Stage is white, but it can be changed as required. The background colour will appear in any part of the finished movie that is not covered by other objects on the Stage. To set the background colour for a movie:

The Stage
colour will act
as the default
background for
the whole of a
movie. If the colour is
changed at any point in the
movie this will be reflected
in the rest of the file too.

1 Select Background Color from the Movie Properties dialog box

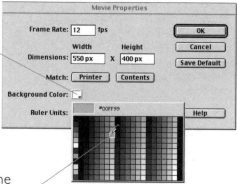

2 Select a colour from the Colour palette. This will be the new background colour for the whole of the Stage

The Stage grid

It is possible to superimpose a grid over the Stage, to enable exact positioning and sizing of objects that are placed there. The grid is only visible in the authoring environment and it does not appear in the final, published movie. To select the grid settings:

Make sure there is a good contrast between the colour of the grid and the Stage background. Otherwise the grid will not be clearly visible, which rather defeats the purpose of having it there.

1 Select View>Grid> Edit Grid from the menu bar

To display the grid on the Stage, select View>Grid> Show Grid from the menu bar, or click here:

2 Select a colour for the grid by clicking here and selecting a colour from the palette that appears

For the grid to be at its most effective, the Snap option has to be turned on. This means that items aligned with the grid will automatically 'snap' to the nearest grid line, for precise alignment.
To activate this, click here:

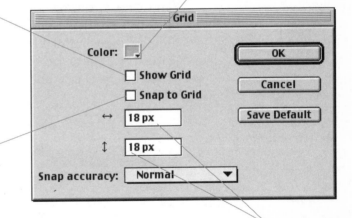

Rulers can also be displayed on the Stage, by selecting View> Rulers from the menu bar.

3 Select the spacing for the grid lines by entering it here. The measurement value is the same as in the Ruler Units box

The Toolbars

The Flash toolbars are collections of buttons that offer quick access to several of the editing and drawing functions within the program. The toolbars differ slightly between the Windows and the Mac versions of Flash:

Mac toolbars

The tools in the Drawing toolbar are looked at in more detail in Chapter Three.

The Mac toolbars consist of only the Drawing toolbar and the Controller toolbar. The Drawing toolbar contains all of the tools required to draw objects in Flash and the Controller toolbar is used to play through a movie while it is being edited in the authoring environment.

The Mac toolbars are accessed by selecting Window>Tools (for the Drawing toolbar) or Window>Controller

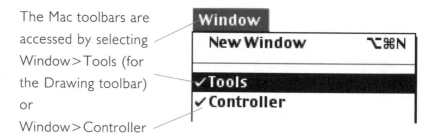

Windows toolbars

The Standard toolbar has icons that act as shortcuts for commonly used items on the Menu bar, such as Open, New, Save and Print. The Status bar denotes whether Caps Lock and Num Lock are on.

In addition to the Drawing and the Controller toolbars, the Windows version of Flash also has a Standard toolbar and a Status bar. These are accessed by selecting View from the Menu bar and then checking on the appropriate option.

The Standard toolbar

The Status bar

The Menu bar

The Menu bar provides access to the core elements of Flash for editing movies. This is located at the top of the program and covers all of the functions that are required to create, edit and test a Flash movie.

If a menu item has a right-pointing arrow after it, this means that there is a sub-menu linked to the main item. Click on the arrow to view the sub-menu.

The File menu

This contains menus for basic functions such as opening and saving movies and setting preferences for editing and publishing.

The Edit menu

This contains commands for editing items within a movie (e.g. Copy and Paste, selection tools and inserting objects).

The elements of each menu will be looked at in greater detail as they occur throughout the book.

The View menu

This gives you control of how your movie looks on screen. This includes showing and hiding items and viewing movies at different magnifications.

The Insert menu

This allows you to manipulate objects, layers and frames.

The Modify menu

This is used to access dialog boxes affecting the properties of items such as layers, scenes and the whole movie. It also provides for some general formatting.

Menus that only apply to specific items are also available in Flash. These are known as contextual menus and they show the options that are available for a particular item. This can be anything within the Flash window.

These menus can be accessed by moving the cursor over the item whose contextual menu you want to see. Then right-click (Windows) or Ctrl+click (Mac) and the menu connected with that item will appear.

The Text menu

This provides options for formatting text.

The Control menu

This lets you test your movie and see how various parts of it, or the whole thing, will look when it is played back.

The Window menu

This determines how the open windows are displayed, gives access to the Panels and, on the Mac, gives access to the toolbars.

The Help menu

This provides online help in the form of Balloon Help and also the Flash help topics, lessons and samples.

Panels

Panels are an element of Flash that give additional information about various items that are on the Stage. There are five main Panels and they are all accessed by selecting Window>Panels and then selecting the relevant Panel. By default the Panels are grouped together as follows:

Info

This contain the following Panels:

- Info, which contains information about the currently selected item on the Stage.

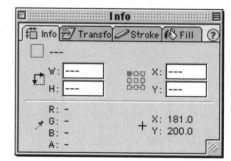

- Transform, which enables you to rotate and skew objects.

- Stroke, which has options for changing the appearance of lines.

- Fill, which has options for changing the fill colour of an object.

Mixer

This contains the following Panels:

- Mixer, which can be used to create custom colours for use in a movie.

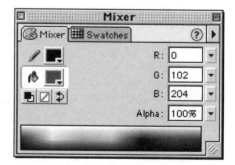

- Swatches, which can be used to select colours and gradients from a colour palette.

Symbols and instances are techniques used by Flash to minimise the size of graphics in a movie. They are looked at in greater detail in Chapter Six.

Frames are used in Flash to insert content at different parts of a movie and create an animated effect. This can be done automatically by using an animation technique called tweening.

Frames are looked at in greater detail in Chapter Eight and animation and tweening are covered in Chapter Nine.

The final Panel (not shown here) is the Generator one. This is another Macromedia product that can be used to create dynamic Web content. More information about the Generator can be found at:

• http://www.macromedia. com/generator

(There are no spaces in the address.)

Instance

This contain the following Panels:

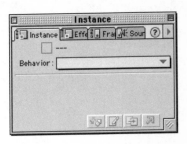

- Instance, which contains information about the currently select instance on the Stage.

- Frame, which displays any names which have been given to a frame and whether any tweening has been applied.

- Sounds, which has options for modifying any sounds that have been added to a movie.

- Effects, which can be used to change the colour attributes of an instance.

Character

This contain the following Panels:

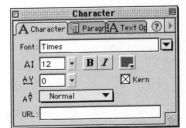

- Character, which allows you to select a font, size and formatting, such as bold and italics.

- Paragraph, which has options for aligning text

- Text options, which allows you to specify the type of fonts used.

Scene

This contains one Panel:

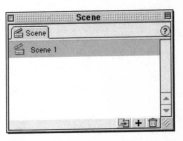

- Scene, which contains details about the current scene being worked on within the movie.

Viewing options

During the editing process it is important to be able to view the contents of the Stage at different magnifications. On some occasions you will want to zoom in on objects to edit them or position them precisely, while on others you will want to view the entire Stage so you can see how various elements appear in relation to others. This can be done by using either the View menu or the Zoom tool.

View menu
This allows you to select various magnification levels for viewing the Stage:

On the magnification menu, show Frame displays the objects on the Stage and Show All displays the objects on the Stage and the Work Area, at the most appropriate size.

1 Select View > Magnification from the Menu bar

2 Select a magnification size

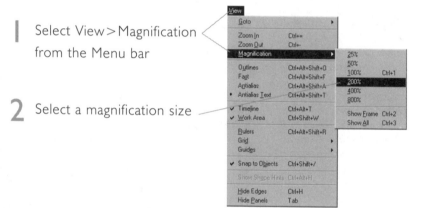

Zoom tool
This can be used to magnify a certain part of the Stage.

Magnify an object on the Stage by clicking on it once with the Zoom tool. Or click and drag so that a rectangle is drawn around the object. The items inside will be magnified.

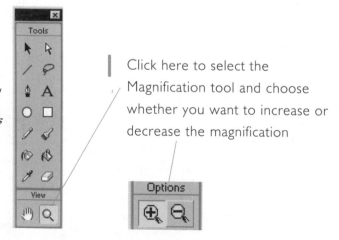

Click here to select the Magnification tool and choose whether you want to increase or decrease the magnification

Creating objects

This chapter looks at the basics of drawing objects in Flash and gives an overview of the contents of the Drawing toolbar.

Covers

Chapter Three

Drawing in Flash

One of the most powerful elements of Flash is its drawing tools. At first sight these may seem as if they are capable of little more than creating a variety of lines and shapes, such as circles and squares. However, these tools are a lot more versatile than this and, with practise and a small degree of artistic flair, they can be used to create an array of stunning graphical images. Before you get started with creating objects with the drawing tools there are a few areas to look at that have a major impact on drawing operations in Flash.

Stage level and overlay level objects

Simple objects are created in Flash with one of the drawing tools on the Stage. At this point they are in their most basic form and are known as 'stage level objects' i.e. they are placed directly on the Stage. However, it is also possible to convert objects into 'overlay level objects'. This in effect places them on a transparent film just above the Stage. To the naked eye, a stage level object and an overlay level object are identical. However, they both act differently within the Flash environment:

- Stage level objects are more versatile for editing purposes

- Stage level objects always reside on the Stage and they are covered by anything that is placed on top of them

Overlay objects are created by grouping together two or more drawing objects. For instance, if you have created an image of a wall with dozens of rectangles as the bricks, this can be grouped together to make a single item. This is done by selecting Modify>Group from the Menu bar. Once objects have been grouped together they become a single overlay object.

Overlay objects can also be created by converting graphics into 'symbols'. This is discussed in greater detail in Chapter Six.

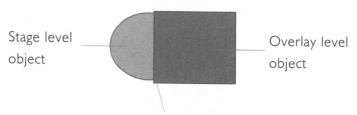

Stage level object   Overlay level object

Within the same layer, overlay level objects will always cover stage level ones

...cont'd

If you want to convert an overlay level object back to a stage level one, perhaps for editing purposes, this can be done by selecting the object and selecting Modify>Break Apart from the Menu bar.

• Stage level objects can interact with each other, i.e. one stage level object can be placed over another similar object and, if the first one is moved, the covered portion of the second object is then cut away:

1 Draw two stage level objects, with parts of them overlapping

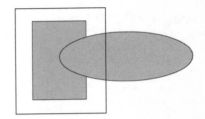

2 Select the Arrow tool and click and drag to select part of both objects

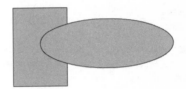

Several stage level objects can overlap on the Stage without affecting each other, if they are created on separate layers. Layers are looked at in greater detail in Chapter Eight.

3 Drag away the selected portion. This interaction between shapes can only be done with stage level objects. Since overlay level objects reside on a different level they do not actually 'touch' stage level ones

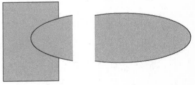

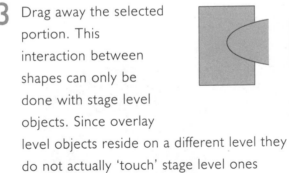

• Stage level objects are usually used when creating new graphics, while overlay level ones are used for the final version of the image

Strokes and fills

Solid objects drawn in Flash, such as circles and squares, are created by using an outline and a fill. In Flash terminology, these are known as strokes and fills respectively. Strokes and fills can be specified before a shape is created, or they can be edited at any time during the creation of the movie. Both stage level and overlay level objects can have their strokes and fills edited independently of each other.

Various drawing tools can be used to create and edit strokes and fills and these will be looked at throughout this chapter.

Fills can be plain colours, shades or even coloured lines to create a rainbow effect. These special effects can be particularly useful when creating buttons that the user will press to trigger an interactive function within a movie.

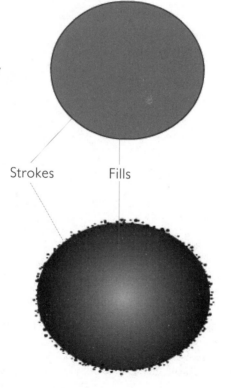

Strokes Fills

An object with a plain colour fill and the default stroke – a solid black line with a weight of I

By changing the fill and stroke attributes, the object is changed considerably

If the fill of a stage level object is selected, it appears shaded. If the stroke is selected it appears as a thick striped line.

Selecting stage level and overlay level objects

Techniques for selecting objects will be looked at in the next chapter but there is one important point to make about selecting solid objects such as circles and squares:

- Overlay level objects can be selected by clicking on them once. The object then appears with a solid outline around it. The whole object can then be moved by clicking and dragging

The stroke of an oval stage level object can be selected by clicking exactly on it once. However, only one side of a rectangular stage level object can be selected at a time. To select all sides, select one side, then hold down Shift and select the other three. Or, double-click on one side.

An overlay object that has been selected. The whole object can now be moved by clicking and dragging

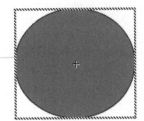

- Stage level objects are selected by clicking on either the stroke or the fill of the object. This can then be moved in the same way as above, except that only the selected element will move, i.e. either the stroke or the fill. If you want to move the whole of a stage level object, the stroke and the fill have to be selected together. This can be done by clicking above and to the left of the object and drawing a rectangle around the object so that it is all selected. It can then be moved by clicking and dragging

If the fill of a stage level object is selected and moved, it will do so without the stroke, and vice versa. They have to both be selected to move together.

A stage level object selected by clicking and dragging with the Arrow tool from the top left of the object. The whole object can now be moved by clicking and dragging. (This is also how stage level objects are grouped)

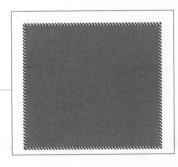

The Drawing toolbar

All of the graphics created with the drawing tools are vector-based graphics. This means they are formed by mathematical equations rather than coloured dots (pixels). This gives the images a smoother appearance and they retain their original quality if they are resized.

The Drawing toolbar contains all of the tools needed to create graphics in Flash and they correspond to what you might find in an artist's studio: brushes, pencils, erasers and colour palettes. The Drawing toolbar has options to enhance individual tools, such as line straightening with the Arrow tool. In addition the Panels can also be used to modify the selection made on the Drawing toolbar e.g. the Stroke Panel can be used to select the line style, weight and colour of the Line, Oval, Rectangle and Pencil tools.

The functions of the Text tool are dealt with separately, in Chapter Five.

One of the most useful options is the one for straightening or smoothing freehand lines. This is looked at in detail in relation to the Pencil tool, on page 40.

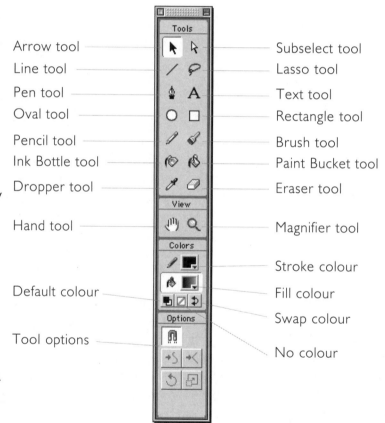

Arrow tool — Subselect tool
Line tool — Lasso tool
Pen tool — Text tool
Oval tool — Rectangle tool
Pencil tool — Brush tool
Ink Bottle tool — Paint Bucket tool
Dropper tool — Eraser tool
Hand tool — Magnifier tool
— Stroke colour
Default colour — Fill colour
— Swap colour
Tool options — No colour

The options are specific to whichever tool is selected. In this example the options are for the Srrow tool. They include snap to grid, line straightening or smoothing, rotating and resizing.

Line tool

The Line tool can be used to draw either straight or diagonal lines. It has no options but the line colour, style and weight can all be set in the Stroke Panel :

Select the
Line tool and
click here to
select a
colour

*In the Line
Thickness box
the first option
is Hairline and
it is the
thinnest line that can be
used.*

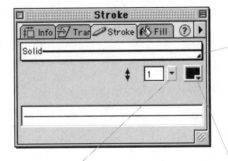

In the Stroke Panel click
here for the Line Style
options

*Once you have
chosen your
options for a
line, it can be
drawn on the
Stage by clicking and
dragging. The Line tool can
be used to create either
straight or diagonal lines.*

Click here for the
Line Thickness
options. This is
operated using a
sliding scale to
increase the
thickness of the line

Click here for the
Line Colour
options.

Pen tool

The Pen tool is one of the new features in Flash 5 and it works in the same way as the Pen tools in other Macromedia programs such as Freehand and Fireworks.

The Pen tool creates lines and curves but it does so by creating precise paths with specific points that allow for precise editing. The Pen tool has no options.

There are preferences for the Pen tool which can be set by selecting Edit>Preferences>Editing from the Menu bar. The preferences are:

- *Show Pen Preview, which displays a preview of the line segment as you move the cursor around the Stage*

- *Show Solid Points, which displays select points on a line as hollow and unselected ones as solid*

- *Show Precise Cursors, which displays the Pen cursor as a crosshair, for greater drawing accuracy.*

When the Pen tool is selected it will continue to add lines to the ones that have previously been drawn. To finish drawing a particular line and move onto another, double-click at the point where you want the line to stop.

Drawing a straight line with the Pen tool

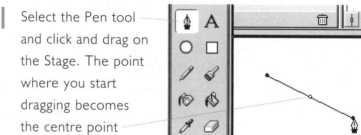

1 Select the Pen tool and click and drag on the Stage. The point where you start dragging becomes the centre point

2 The two points at the ends of the line are known as anchor points

Drawing a curved line with the Pen tool

1 Draw a straight line as above. With the Pen tool still selected click one of the anchor points and drag in the opposite direction to where you want the curve

2 The curve is created according to length and degree to which the anchor points are dragged

Subselect tool

The Subselect tool is another new addition in Flash 5. It is used primarily in conjunction with the Pen tool, but it can also be used to edit lines created with the Pencil, Brush, Line, Oval and Rectangle tools. The Subselect tool has no modifiers and its main use is to edit lines that have been created as paths.

Creating a curved path from a straight line

Using the Subselect tool to select and edit lines can give greater accuracy and versatility than trying to do the same thing with the Arrow tool.

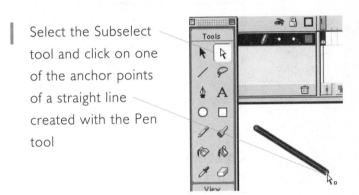

1 Select the Subselect tool and click on one of the anchor points of a straight line created with the Pen tool

2 Drag the anchor point to create a curved path

To revert to a straight line, reverse the process.

The Subselect tool can also be used to modify enclosed shapes, such as rectangles and ovals, or shapes that have been created with the Pen tool.

Oval tool

To draw perfect circles, hold down the Shift key while dragging the Oval tool crosshair.

This is similar to the Line tool in that it has no options of its own and the line style, weight and colour can be determined in the Stroke Panel. In addition the fill for an oval can be selected from the Fill Panel:

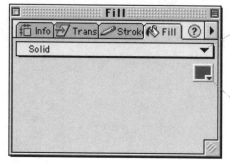

Click here to select the fill style i.e. solid or gradient

Click here to select the fill style i.e. solid or gradient

Once the attributes for a particular drawing tool have been set, they become the default settings for all of the other applicable drawing tools. So if you have set the Oval tool to have a line colour of green, thickness 2, and a fill of dark blue, these will be the settings if you then select another drawing tool, such as the Rectangle tool.

Creating outline and solid ovals

By default, ovals are created with both a line around them and a fill. However, it is possible to create them with only one of these attributes:

1 To create an outline oval, click here on the Fill Colour button

To create an oval with a fill but no line, click on the Stroke Colour button in Step 1 rather than the Fill Colour one. Then select the 'no colour' button as in Step 2.

2 In the colour swatch that appears, click here to set the fill colour to 'no colour'. When the oval is drawn it will only have a line and no fill

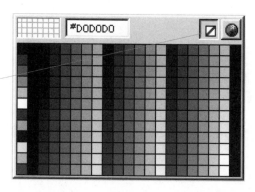

Rectangle tool

The Rectangle tool can be used to draw rectangles and squares. It is similar to the Oval tool, except it has one option, for adding rounded corners to a rectangle:

To draw a perfect square, hold down Shift while you are dragging on the Stage with the Rectangle tool.

| Select the Rectangle tool and click here to access the Rectangle Settings dialog box

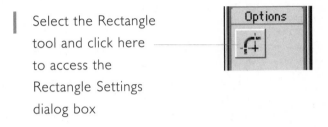

Rectangles can be created with only a stroke or only a fill, in exactly the same way as with ovals on the previous page.

2 Enter a value here to specify how rounded you require the corners of a Rectangle to be

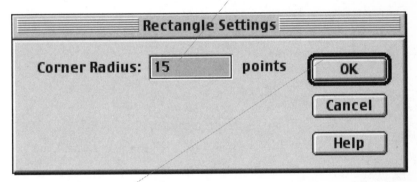

3 Select OK and then draw the rectangle on the Stage

Pencil tool

The Pencil tool is a freehand drawing tool that can be used to create patterns, such as curved lines, or objects such as squares and circles. However, as with most freehand tools in drawing programs, creating objects with the Pencil tool can be an erratic and jerky experience – but only if it is used without any of the assistance that Flash provides for this particular tool. This assistance allows you to specify whether you want your freehand image to be straightened, smoothed or left as it is, with only minor amendments. The Pencil tool does not have any other options, but the line style, weight and colour can be selected in the Stroke Panel in the same way as for the Line tool.

When any line is drawn there will be a slight change in its appearance immediately after it has been finished. This is due to Flash ensuring that the finished line will appear as smooth as possible when viewed in the final movie.

Creating lines with the Pencil tool

Lines that have already been drawn can be straightened or smoothed using the Arrow tool. See page 47

Select the Pencil tool and draw a freehand shape on the Stage

or

Select the Pencil tool and click on the Pencil Mode option button. Select either the Straighten or Smooth option to enable the Pencil tool to automatically straighten or smooth any lines that are drawn

The third option is the Pencil Mode Ink mode. This does not apply any straightening or smoothing and reproduces the line as it is drawn. This option should be used if no assistance is required when drawing lines and shapes.

✓ ⌐	Straighten
S	Smooth
⧖	Ink

⌐	Straighten
✓ S	Smooth
⧖	Ink

Using shape recognition

Not only does the Pencil tool straighten or smooth lines, it can also interpret a particular shape you are trying to draw and create a perfect version of it. This can be invaluable if you are trying to draw items such as ovals and rectangles.

Shape recognition only works when drawing circles, ovals and rectangles. If you try to draw a shape such as a triangle, the Pencil tool will try to either straighten or smooth it depending on which settings have been chosen. However, it will not necessarily transform it into a perfect triangle.

Without shape recognition

Shape recognition applied

Setting assistance levels

There are various options that can be selected to determine the level of assistance given to the drawing tools. To set these levels select Edit>Preferences>Editing from the Menu bar:

Shape recognition works best with the Straighten option selected. If the Smooth option is selected then you could end up with a rectangle with rounded edges. With Ink mode selected, there will be no shape recognition.

- *Connect lines* determines how close the end lines of a rectangle or oval have to be before Flash closes them

- *Smooth curves* determines the degree by which curves are smoothed

- *Recognize lines* determines the tolerance for a line before it is automatically straightened

- *Recognize* sets the tolerance before a shape is turned into an oval or a rectangle

- *Click accuracy* sets the accuracy for selecting strokes

Brush tool

The Brush tool creates broad brush strokes that give the effect of lines being created by actual paintbrushes. The options for the Brush tool are:

- Brush Mode

- Brush Size

- Brush Shape

- Lock Fill

Click here to select the brush mode (see tip)

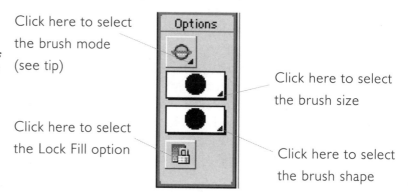

Click here to select the brush size

Click here to select the Lock Fill option

Click here to select the brush shape

To use the Brush tool, draw a shape on the Stage as if you were using a paintbrush or a thick crayon. Click and drag to create a line with the Brush tool. You can release the mouse and then draw another line: as long as it is touching the first line, and is the same colour, it will become part of the same shape. This way you can build up complex shapes using a variety of lines. You can even change the brush size and shape halfway through and the new lines will become part of the original object, as long as they are touching it. Brush stokes are objects rather than true strokes.

The Lock Fill option can be used if you are using a gradient or a bitmap as a brush stroke fill. Select the Brush tool then select a gradient/bitmap. You can then draw separate shapes on the Stage and the fill will change in each one, giving the effect of the gradient/bitmap in a disjointed pattern.

Ink Bottle tool

The Ink Bottle tool can be used to add an outline (stroke) to an object that does not have one, or to change the attributes of an existing outline. This only applies to stage level objects. The line colour, weight and style can be selected in the Stroke Panel. There are no options for the Ink Bottle tool. To use the Ink Bottle tool:

Ink bottle attributes can be applied to outlines of elements within an object. However, the new line attributes will only be applied to any elements within the object that can support an outline. For instance, if you had a face graphic and clicked inside it with the Ink Bottle tool, elements such as the eyes, nose and mouth would have the selected outline attributes applied to them.

1 Select the Ink Bottle tool and then select the required line colour, weight and style in the Stroke Panel

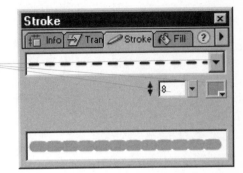

2 Position the Ink Bottle icon over the area where you want to add or edit the line. Click once to apply the new attributes

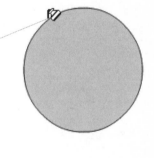

Paint Bucket tool

Fill colours can also be selected and mixed in the Mixer and Swatches Panels.

The Paint Bucket tool can be used to create a coloured fill within an object, or it can change an existing fill. The fill colour can be selected in the Fill Panel:

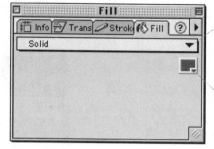

Click here to select the fill style i.e. solid or gradient

Click here to select the fill colour

The Gap Size modifier specifies how the Paint Bucket fills objects whose outlines are not complete. The settings are:

- *Don't Close Gaps, which prevents a fill being applied to an object with a gap in its outline*

- *Close Small Gaps, which adds a fill to an object with small gaps in its outline*

- *Close Medium Gaps, which adds a fill to an object with medium gaps in its outline, and;*

- *Close Large Gaps, which adds a fill to an object with large gaps in its outline*

The only option for the Paint Bucket tool is the Gap Size (see tip)

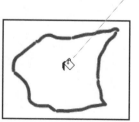

Click here to select the gap size options

To use the Paint Bucket tool, select a fill colour and position the paint bucket over the object to be filled or whose fill is to be edited. Click once to add the new fill:

The gap size tolerance can alter depending on the magnification of the screen.

Dropper tool

The Dropper tool only works on stage level objects and it allows you to take the fill or stroke attributes of one item and transfer them to another. It has no modifiers. To use the Dropper tool:

1 Select the Dropper tool and Position it over the fill or stroke that you want to copy. Click once to load the Dropper tool

If you want to transfer the stroke attributes from one object to another, click once on its outline with the Dropper tool. If you want to transfer the fill, then click once on that.

2 The Dropper tool then activates either the Paint Bucket tool or the Line tool, depending on whether the dropper was loaded with the fill or the stroke of an object

3 Click once on the selected object to transfer the fill or stroke from the original object

The Dropper tool can also be used to capture bitmap images so that they can be used as fills.

The tools underneath the Dropper tool on the Drawing toolbar are the Hand and the Zoom tools. The Zoom tool is looked at on page 28 and the Hand tool can be used to move around the Stage by clicking and dragging while the Hand tool is selected.

Eraser tool

The Eraser tool can be used to delete items on the Stage. It can be used on both strokes and fills, but it can only be applied to stage level objects. The options for the Eraser tool are:

- Eraser Shape
- Faucet
- Eraser Mode

The Eraser tool is activated by selecting it from the toolbar and then clicking and dragging over the Stage. When you are using the Eraser tool it may appear as if it is deleting everything it touches rather than following the specifications of the Eraser mode modifiers. However, when the mouse is released, only the specified elements will have been deleted. (Any other items will reappear.)

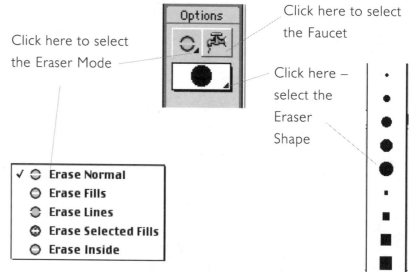

Click here to select the Eraser Mode

Click here to select the Faucet

Click here – select the Eraser Shape

The Faucet option for the Eraser tool can be used to delete an entire outline or fill with a single click. Select the Faucet modifier, then click once on a line or fill. This removes it from the Stage.

If the Eraser tool is applied to overlay level objects, it will have no effect.

The options for Eraser Mode are:

- *Erase Normal*, which erases both strokes and fills
- *Erase Fills*, which only erases fills, even if the eraser passes over a stroke
- *Erase Lines*, which only erases strokes, even if the eraser passes over a fill
- *Erase Selected Fills*, which only erases fills that have first been selected. Everything else is untouched
- *Erase Inside*, which only erases inside an area without affecting the stroke

Arrow tool

The Arrow tool is the first one on the Drawing toolbar and its purpose is to select objects on the Stage. Some simple selection techniques for stage level and overlay level objects were shown on page 33 and Chapter Four covers some of the other ways to select and then manipulate objects in Flash. The options for the Arrow tool are:

All of the Arrow tool options, except Snap, are only active if an object has already been selected. Otherwise they are greyed out.

- Snap

- Smooth

- Straighten

- Rotate

- Scale

The Snap option can be used to align objects with the grid on the Stage.
To show the grid, select View>Grid>Show Grid so there is a tick showing next to it. Objects can then be placed on the lines of the grid and the Snap modifier will ensure that they are aligned exactly on the grid line.

Click here to select the Snap option

Click here to select the Smooth option

Click here to select the Rotate option

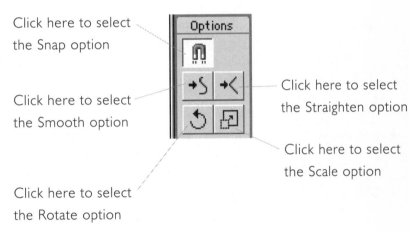

Click here to select the Straighten option

Click here to select the Scale option

The Smooth and Straighten options are used in relation to editing lines (see page 54) and the Rotate and Scale options are used to change the orientation and size of objects (see pages 57–60).

Lasso tool

The Lasso tool is also a selection tool. However, it makes selections by using freehand techniques rather than the point and click or dragging selection employed by the Arrow tool. For instance, it could be used to make a selection of the outline of an open hand. The options for the Lasso tool are:

As with the Arrow tool, the Lasso tool can employ several selection methods and these are looked at in greater detail in Chapter Four.

- Magic Wand

- Magic Wand Properties

- Polygon Mode

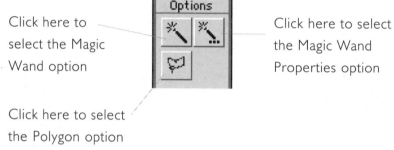

Click here to select the Magic Wand option

Click here to select the Magic Wand Properties option

Click here to select the Polygon option

The Lasso tool can be used to select segments of stage level objects but not overlay level ones.

The Magic Wand option can be used so that the Lasso tool can make selections based on the colour of objects. Its settings can be altered using the Magic Wand Properties option. This is looked at on page 78.

The Polygon option can be used to draw polygon shapes around objects by connecting two points, stopping, and then connecting another two points until the required object has been selected. This can be very useful if you want to select a large, irregular object but your hand is not steady enough to draw around it freehand.

Editing objects

This chapter looks at some of the editing functions that can be applied to drawing objects in Flash. It covers selecting items; editing lines and fills; resizing and reshaping objects; Copy and Paste; aligning items; changing the stacking order; and creating cut-aways.

Covers

Chapter Four

Selecting with the Arrow tool

Clicking and click-dragging

In Chapter Three it was shown how the Arrow tool could be used to select both stage level and overlay level objects and this can be done as follows:

In Flash, an outline is a line that has no end i.e. around an oval or a rectangle. A line, in a Flash context, has a specific beginning and end.

- Click once on an overlay level object to select it

- Click once on the fill of a stage level object to select it

- Click once on the outline of a stage level oval to select it or double-click on a stage level rectangle

- Double-click within a stage level object to select both the fill and the outline

If two or more stage level objects of the same colour are touching, they will all become selected even if only one of the objects is clicked on. For instance, if two squares with a blue fill and no outline were touching they could both be selected by clicking once on either object.

- Click and drag around either a stage level object or an overlay level object to select the whole object

The Arrow tool can also be used to select multiple objects, of all types, on the Stage by clicking and dragging:

1 Select the Arrow tool

2 Click and drag a rectangle around the items to be selected

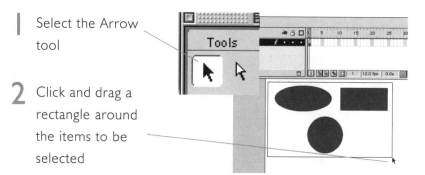

3 Release the mouse and all of the items become selected

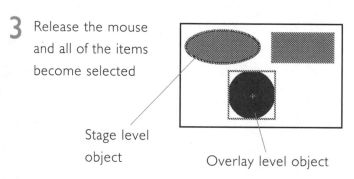

Stage level object

Overlay level object

Selecting lines

Since lines in Flash are based on vectors (mathematical equations) rather than being composed of dots, it is possible to select different parts as well as the whole thing. This can be useful if you want to edit one specific part of a line. Lines drawn with the Line tool or the Pencil tool can be selected this way, but only if they are stage level objects. When a line is created in Flash the vector calculation creates a corner point and a curve point for each segment of the line. The curve point is between two corner points and this is the segment of a line that can be select by clicking on it. To select part of a line:

To select more than one segment of a line, hold down Shift and click on the segments you want to select. This is the default setting but it can be changed so that multiple segments can be selected just by clicking on them.

To change the default, select Edit>Preferences> General from the Menu bar and check off the Selection Options: Shift Select box.

Although the Brush tool can be used to create what appears to be lines, these are in fact blocks of colour. You cannot select a segment by clicking on it. However, parts of brush stroke objects can be selected by clicking and dragging – see overleaf.

The Subselect tool can also be used to edit lines. To do this, click once on a line to select the whole line. Then click and drag on the markers that appear on the line to alter the appearance of it.

1 Select the Arrow tool; place it at the start of the line. This is the first corner point, denoted by a right angle next to the cursor

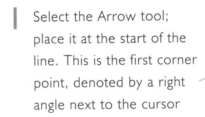

2 Move the cursor along the line. A small curve will appear next to the cursor, denoting it is a curve point

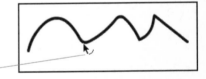

3 When the cursor finds the next corner point the right angle reappears. This area is a line segment

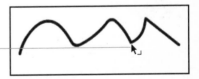

4 Click once anywhere on the segment to select it

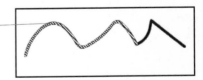

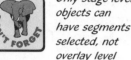

Only stage level objects can have segments selected, not overlay level ones.

Selecting parts of objects

In addition to selecting complete objects and segments of lines, it is also possible to use the Arrow tool to select parts of an object. This can be useful if you want to edit a portion of an object:

When clicking and dragging to select part of an object, position the cursor outside the object to begin the operation. Otherwise you may select the object's fill or outline.

| With the Arrow tool selected click and drag to create the area within the object you want to edit

2 The selected area can now be edited – for instance, changing its colour fill with the Paint Bucket or Brush tools

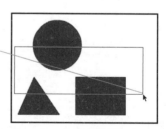

This technique can also be used to select parts of several different objects:

If selected objects are grouped they become a single item as an overlay level object. For more on grouping, see page 55.

| Click and drag to create the selection area

2 The selected objects, or areas of objects, become shaded to indicate they are selected. They can then be edited, grouped or moved

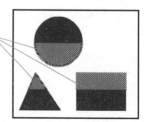

Selecting with the Lasso tool

Selections with the Lasso tool have to have the same starting and ending point.

While the Arrow tool can be used to select objects by clicking on them or drawing symmetrical boxes around them, the Lasso tool is better for selecting irregular shapes. This can be done by creating a freehand selection or one using the Polygon option.

Freehand selection

| Select the Lasso tool. The options do not have to be selected

When making a freehand selection, keep the mouse button pressed down until you want to finish the process. If you let go of it before you come back to the starting point, the selection will not be made.

2 Trace around the object to be selected. Finish the selection by double-clicking at the point where you began the selection

Polygon selection

| Select the Lasso tool and the Polygon option

The Lasso tool can also be used to select colours within bitmap objects. This is looked at in more detail in Chapter Five.

2 Click on a starting point and drag out a line. Release the mouse button where you want the line to end. Repeat this until the whole shape is enclosed by these lines

Editing lines

In addition to using the Pencil, Smooth and Straighten options to create lines with these properties, it is also possible to apply these attributes to lines that have already been created. This is done by using the Arrow tool and its options:

1 Select the Arrow tool and select the line to be edited

If a line consists of more than one segment, double-click on it to select the whole line.

2 Select either the Smooth option or the Straighten one

3 Each click on the options button produces an incremental change in the line:

In Windows, once a line, or line segment, is selected, the Straighten and Smooth options are also available on the Standard toolbar.

After 2 clicks on Smooth

After 10 clicks on Smooth

After 2 clicks on Straighten

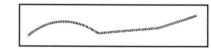

After 10 clicks on Straighten

Grouping objects

Several individual objects can be grouped together to form a new, single object. Groups can consist of any objects on the Stage, including stage level objects, overlay level objects, bitmaps and text. Creating groups is useful for applying the same editing technique to multiple items simultaneously, such as moving or resizing. To group objects:

1 Use the Arrow tool to select the items you want to group, either by shift-clicking or by dragging and drawing around them

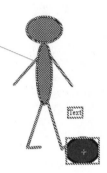

2 Select Modify>Group in the Menu bar

3 A thick shaded border appears around the grouped objects

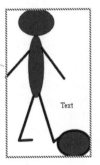

4 Double-click on the group to edit individual items within it. The other items on the Stage are greyed out and the group is identified here

Moving objects

Even if the greatest care is taken when placing objects on the Stage, it is inevitable that most items will have to be moved at some point during the editing process. This can either be done manually or by using the Info panel.

Objects can also be moved by selecting them, then pressing the directional arrow keys. This moves the object one pixel at a time. To speed up this process, hold down Shift and press the arrow keys. This will move the object eight pixels each time.

Moving manually

1 Select View in the Menu bar and check on both Show Grid and Snap to Grid

2 Select the object to be moved and drag it to its new location

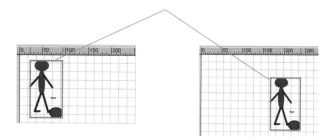

Moving with the Info panel

When using the Info panel to move objects it is a good idea to have the rulers showing. This allows you to see the coordinates of where the object is currently situated and also where it will appear once new values have been entered.

To view the rulers, select View>Rulers from the Menu bar.

1 Select the object to be moved and select Window>Panels>Info

2 Enter values in the 'X' and 'Y' boxes to move the object. Click here if you want the coordinates to refer to the middle of the object

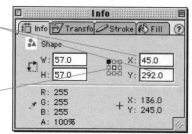

Resizing objects

As with positioning objects, it is frequently the case that items within a movie have to be resized (also known as scaling in Flash). This could be to increase or decrease an object's prominence on the Stage or to change its proportions in relation to other objects around it. Flash provides three ways to resize objects on the Stage and these apply equally to stage level and overlay level objects.

Resizing manually

If an object is already selected, the resizing function can also be accessed by selecting Modify>Transform>Scale from the Menu bar.

1 Select an object with the Arrow tool (this can include one or more objects)

2 The Arrow tool should still be selected. Select the Scale option

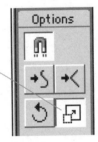

Click and drag on one of the resizing handles in the middle of a line to resize the object either horizontally or vertically. Click on one of the corner handles to resize it both horizontally and vertically in equal proportions.

3 Click on one of the eight resizing handles.

4 When a double headed arrow appears, drag to resize the object

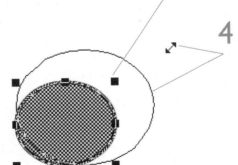

If several objects have been selected, they will all be resized proportionally.

Resizing with a dialog box

Resizing using the Scale and Rotate dialog box is a useful option if you want to scale an object precisely. For instance, if you want to make an object half its original size then the most accurate way would be to enter 50% as a value in this dialog box.

1 Select an object and select Modify> Transform>Scale and Rotate from the Menu bar

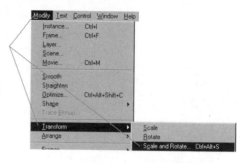

2 Enter a percentage value for the increase/decrease amount. Select OK

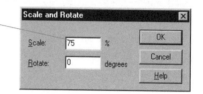

Resizing with the Transform panel

If the Constrain box is checked on in the Transform panel then the height and width will be set to the same values for both whenever a new value is entered.

1 Select an object and select Window> Panels>Transform

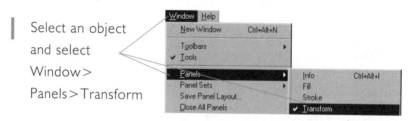

Click here to make a copy of the original object, at the same time as you resize it.

2 Enter values here for the new width and height for the object. Press Return or Enter to apply the changes

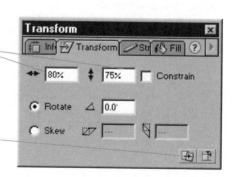

Rotating and skewing objects

An object can be rotated (moved to varying degrees around its centre point) or skewed (distorted at various angles along its horizontal or vertical axis). The operations for doing this are similar to those for resizing objects and they can be applied to stage level or overlay level objects. However, overlay level objects can be rotated in a slightly different fashion (see the tip).

Stage level objects are always rotated around their actual centre point, which remains static. However, the centre point of overlay level objects can be moved, to change the point from where the rotation is applied.

To do this, select an overlay object, then select Modify>Transform>Edit Center from the Menu bar. A thick cross appears in the middle of the object. Click and drag to move it around the object and set a new centre point.

Rotating manually

1 Select an object and select the Arrow tool and the Rotate option.

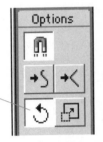

2 Click on one of the corner rotating handles and drag the object to its new position (dragging one of the side handles will distort the object i.e. skew it)

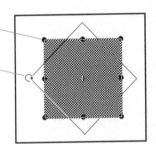

Rotating with a dialog box

1 Select an object and select Modify>Transform>Scale and Rotate, in the same way as for resizing an object

2 Enter a value for the amount you want the object to be rotated

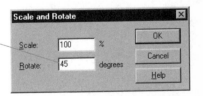

Skewing with the Transform panel

1 Select an object and select Window> Panels>Transform from the Menu bar

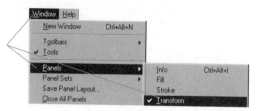

2 Check on the Skew button and enter horizontal or vertical values for skewing the object

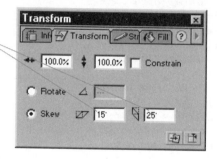

3 The skew effect makes the object look misshapen

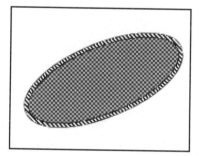

Rapid rotation and flipping

Objects can be re-orientated quickly by rotating them left or right by 90 degrees or flipping them 180 degrees horizontally or vertically. To do this:

Select an object and select Modify> Transform and any of the following commands:

 The Transform menu also has an option for undoing any resizing or rotating commands that have been applied to objects, but only overlay level ones. To do this, select an overlay level object, then select Modify>Transform>Remove Transform from the Menu bar. The object will now revert to its original state.

This is similar to the Undo option but it can be quicker if several editing commands have been applied, since it takes the object back to its original state in one step.

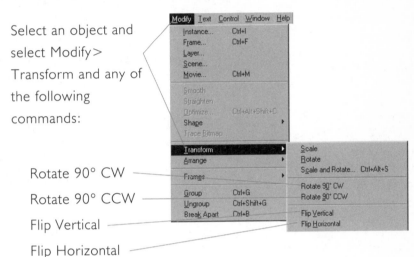

Rotate 90° CW

Rotate 90° CCW

Flip Vertical

Flip Horizontal

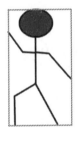

Original

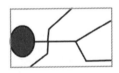

Rotate Left

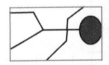

Rotate Right

Flip Vertical

Flip Horizontal

Reshaping objects

Both lines and fills can have their shapes altered, which can be a useful way of manipulating items and creating some interesting freehand effects. When reshaping objects there are three important points to remember:

- You can only reshape stage level objects

- When you are reshaping lines or fills you do not have to select them first. If you do you will move the item rather than reshape it

- Both lines and fills in Flash are made up of corner points and curve points. The corner points are at the end of lines or at a point in a line or fill that Flash calculates is at a sufficient angle. Corner points are denoted by a small right angle next to the cursor when it passes over one. These can be used to reshape the corner of fills or the end of lines. Curve points are denoted by a small curve next to the cursor. These can be used to reshape the middle of fills or lines.

Reshaping a straight line

1 Select the Arrow tool and position it over one end of the line, without selecting the line. A small right angle will appear next to the cursor

2 Click and drag to stretch and reposition the line

Reshaping a curved line

1 Select the Arrow tool and position it over part of the line, without selecting it. A small curve will appear next to the cursor

It is possible to add corner points to fill objects. This gives increased flexibility when reshaping objects and means that corner points can even be added to objects such as perfect circles.

To create corner points: select the Arrow tool and position it over a curve point so the small curve is showing. Hold down Ctrl+click (Windows) or Alt+click (Mac) and then drag the cursor. As it is dragged the object will be reshaped and a new corner point will be created.

2 Click and drag to reshape the curve

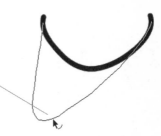

Reshaping a fill

1 Select the Arrow tool and position it over either a corner point or a curve point of the fill object

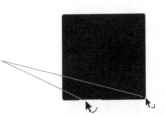

2 Click and drag to reshape the fill

Reshaping using corner points   Reshaping using curve points

Copy and Paste

Copied items can be pasted back into the location they came from as well as a new frame, layer, scene or movie.

In common with many software programs, Flash offers the standard Copy, Paste and Cut facilities. In addition, it has an option for pasting objects into the same relative position as they were copied from. The Copy and Paste functions are particularly useful for copying or moving items between frames, layers and scenes. They can also be used to move items from one movie to another.

Standard Copy and Paste

Edit>Cut can be used in the same way as Edit>Copy. However, this removes the item from its original location, but it can still be pasted somewhere else.

Select the item to be copied

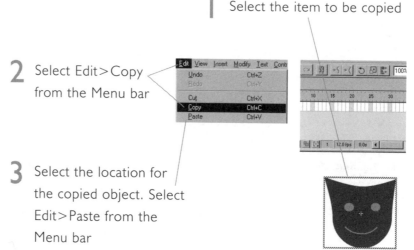

2 Select Edit>Copy from the Menu bar

3 Select the location for the copied object. Select Edit>Paste from the Menu bar

Paste in Place is an excellent option if you want to have various items in exactly the same place throughout a movie. This could include items such as company logos or menu bars.

Using Paste in Place

To paste an object in the same relative position, measured from the top-left corner of the Stage, from where it was copied:

Copy the object as above, choose a location for it, then select Edit> Paste in Place from the Menu bar

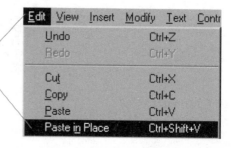

Aligning objects

Even with the grid and ruler options, it can be useful to have a function for aligning a number of objects in one operation – for instance if you want to line up a group of buttons as navigation tools. Flash provides this with a number of alignment options for both stage level and overlay level objects.

Alignment panel

Alignment is done with the Align panel and there are a number of options that can be selected. To align objects:

| Select the objects to be aligned

In addition to aligning objects vertically and horizontally, the Align panel also has options for matching the width and height of the largest object in the selection.

2 Select Windows> Panels>Align from the Menu bar

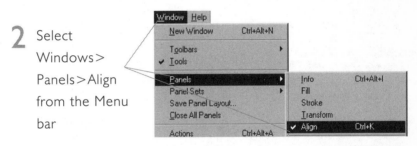

Text can be aligned using the same method as for objects.

3 Select the required alignment options from the Align dialog box (see overleaf)

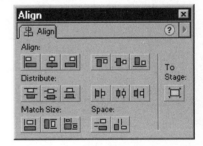

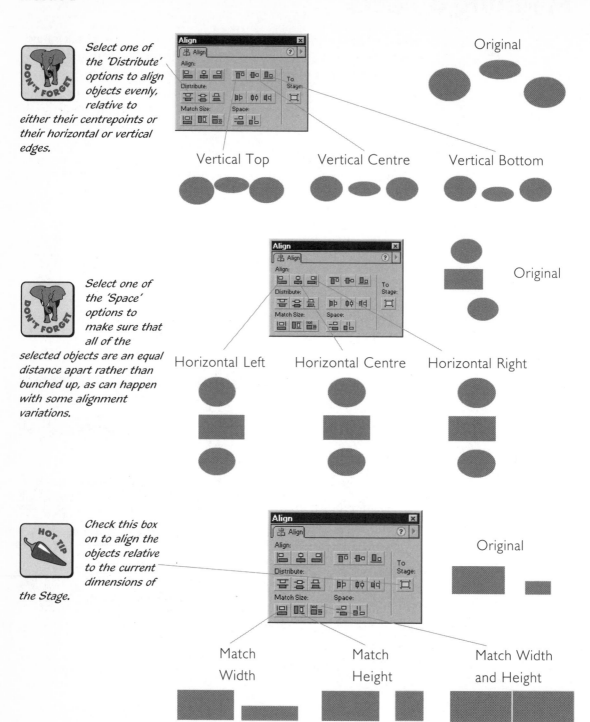

Select one of the 'Distribute' options to align objects evenly, relative to either their centrepoints or their horizontal or vertical edges.

Original

Vertical Top   Vertical Centre   Vertical Bottom

Select one of the 'Space' options to make sure that all of the selected objects are an equal distance apart rather than bunched up, as can happen with some alignment variations.

Original

Horizontal Left   Horizontal Centre   Horizontal Right

Check this box on to align the objects relative to the current dimensions of the Stage.

Original

Match Width   Match Height   Match Width and Height

Stacking order

As movies are created, the number of objects on the Stage increases. This is generally not a problem if the objects are apart, but when they start to overlap it can become an issue. For instance, if you have an image of a person kicking a ball, it is important to have the ball showing in front of the individual rather than behind them. This is known as stacking, and Flash enables you to arrange objects in a variety of ways.

Only overlay objects can be arranged: if you have a stage level object that you want to arrange it has to first be grouped or turned into a symbol (see Chapter Six).

To arrange overlay level items:

1   Select the object whose stacking order you want to change

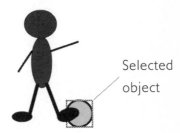

Selected object

2   Select Modify>Arrange from the Menu bar and select one of the stacking options

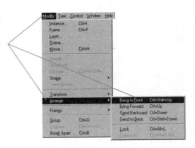

3   The stacking order of the selected object changes accordingly

The object is now to the fore

Cut-aways

If two stage level objects with the same fill or outline colours are placed over each other they will not be able to be used for cut-aways. Instead they will merge into one object: any matching colours in stage level objects that touch, join together as one.

The reason stage level objects cannot be stacked is because they physically affect each other when one is placed on top of another. In this way, one stage level object can be used to create cut-aways from another. This can be done with either objects or lines.

Cut-aways with objects

1 Draw two stage level objects, one on top of the other

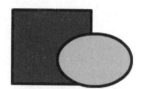

2 Select one object and click and drag it to see the cut-away effect

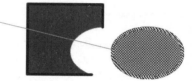

Cut-aways with lines

If you try to use a stage level object to cut away an overlay level one, nothing will happen. Since the overlay object is, in effect, on a different level the stage level one will just appear behind it and no interaction will take place.

1 Draw a stage level object. With either the Line or the Pencil tool, draw a line across it. This divides the object into two distinct segments

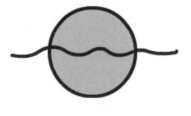

2 Select one of the segments and click and drag it to see the effect of the cut-away

Colour and text

Both colour and text can be used to give extra dimension to a Flash movie. This chapter looks at adding colours and gradients to objects, creating new colours and gradients and selecting colours. It also shows how to add, format and manipulate text.

Covers

Chapter Five

Standard Colour palette

When the Colour Line or Colour Fill box is chosen for a drawing tool the standard Flash Colour palette appears. This has a selection of the most commonly used colours and it contains two elements:

Any of the applicable drawing tools can be loaded with fill or gradient colours. Select the tool you want to use and then select an option from the Colour palette. This will stay in place for any other drawing tools, until another selection is made.

- *Solid colours.* Solid blocks of colour

- *Gradient colours.* Bands of colours that merge into each other to give a gradient effect. Gradient colours can either be radial gradients, which use rings of colours to create the gradient effect, or linear gradients, which use lines of colours

Click here to select a solid colour fill

Radial gradients are excellent for items such as buttons on a Web page. The gradient gives the button greater depth and creates a more interesting 3-D effect.

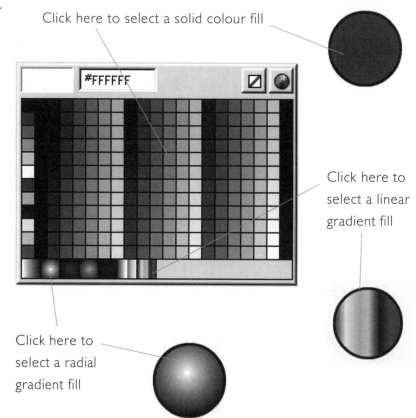

Click here to select a linear gradient fill

Click here to select a radial gradient fill

Adding solid colours

Computer monitors create colours by mixing different amounts of red, green and blue (the RGB colour model). In theory this can produce over 16 million colours. However, not all computer monitors can display this number of colours. The maximum number guaranteed to be displayed correctly is 256 (or only 216) and this is known as the Web Safe Colour palette.

If you use colours outside this range some monitors will interpret them as best they can, but they may differ from the original. This is known as 'dithering' and it usually results in inferior colour representation. If in doubt, stick to Web Safe colours, which are the ones Flash uses by default.

Since not everyone wants to be restricted to just the colours within the standard Colour palette, Flash has an option for creating new colours and adding these to the Colour palette. This gives an almost limitless range of colours from which to choose, but if these are intended for a Web page, it is worth remembering that they may not necessarily be displayed on the user's browser exactly as intended (see the tip).

Creating a new solid colour

Click here on the Colour palette to access the Color dialog box

On a Mac the following Colour Picker is activated

Click here to select the various methods for creating a colour

Click here to select a colour

Colour preview

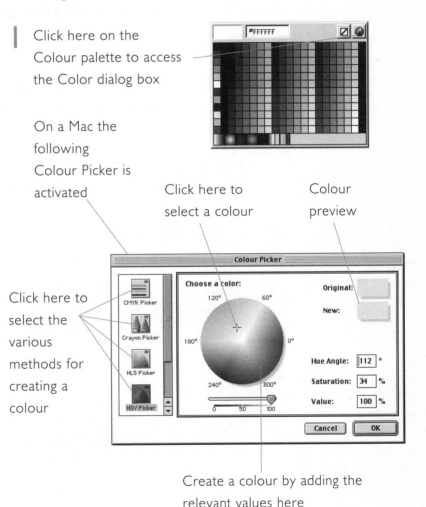

Create a colour by adding the relevant values here

Hexadecimal is a system that uses six digits to denote colours. It works by giving values for red, green and blue, using a base system of sixteen. This uses the numbers 0–9 and the letters A–F. Each of the three colours (Red, Green and Blue) used to create a hexadecimal colour has a combination of two letters/ digits assigned to it.. For instance, white is FFFFFF and black is 000000.

There are 256 (16x16) hexadecimal combinations, matching the Web Safe palette.

In Windows the following Color dialog box is activated

Select a standard colour here

Edit hue/saturation by clicking and dragging this crosshair

Edit brightness by clicking and dragging this slider

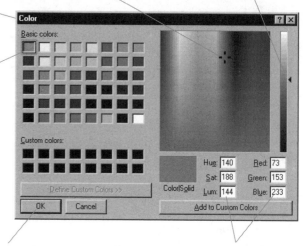

OK once a colour has been created

Create custom colours by entering values in these boxes

Any colour that is created in the Mixer panel is immediately applied as the fill colour or stroke colour (whichever is selected) on the Drawing toolbar.

Creating colours with the Mixer panel

New colours can also be created by using the Mixer panel:

If the Alpha setting for a colour (its transparency) is at 100% then it will be at its most dense. If it is at 0% it will be completely transparent i.e. invisible.

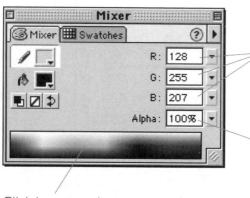

Enter values here for the amount of red, green and blue in the new colour

Enter a value here for the level of transparency of the colour

Click here to select a new colour

Adding gradients

Gradients can be added and edited in a similar way to solid colours. This is done by accessing the Fill panel and selecting which colours will make up the gradient and how thick each band of colour will be.

In addition to accessing the Colour palette by selecting a drawing tool and then selecting the Fill or Line Colour box, it can also be displayed by selecting Window>Colors from the Menu bar.

Creating a new gradient:

1 Select Window> Panels>Fill from the Menu bar

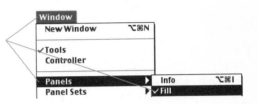

2 Click here to select either a linear or a radial gradient

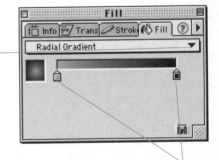

Gradients can produce very effective fills for items such as buttons. However, try not to overdo this effect and use gradients carefully.

3 The colours that make up the gradient are shown here. Click once on one of the pointers to edit a particular colour in the gradient. This can be done by clicking here and selecting a colour from the Colour palette

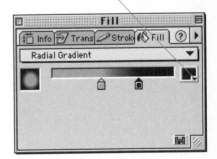

Colours can be removed from gradients by clicking and dragging a gradient pointer off the scale.

4 Drag the pointers to change the amount of each colour in the gradient. The effect is shown in the preview box

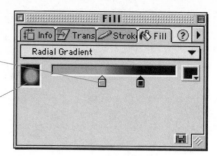

Gradients must have a minimum of two colours. If more colours are used this allows for either dramatic effects to be created with different colours or greater subtlety to be achieved by using several shades in the gradient.

5 Add more pointers by Shift-clicking. The more pointers, the more flexibility there is for editing the gradient

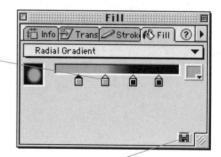

7 Select the Save icon to add the gradient to the Colour palette

Editing gradient fills

Gradients can be applied to objects in the same way as solid colours: select a drawing tool such as the Oval or Rectangle tool, select the Fill box and choose a gradient from the Colour palette. Alternatively, the Paint Bucket can be used to change the gradient of an existing stage level object. It is also possible to use the Paint Bucket tool to edit existing gradient fills.

The Brush tool can be used to create lines with gradient fills. Select the tool and the gradient, as you would with the Oval or the Rectangle tool, and then draw a line on the Stage. In reality, it is a drawing object rather than a true line, which cannot have gradient fills applied.

Moving a gradient's centre point

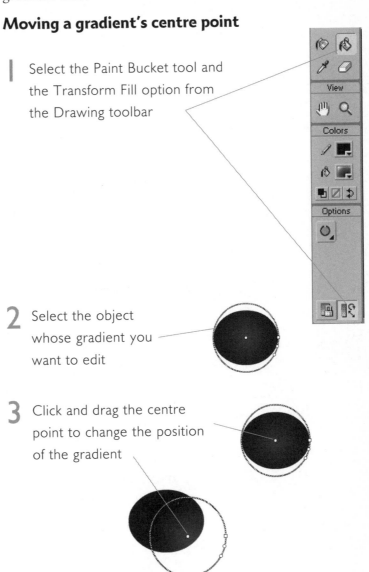

1 Select the Paint Bucket tool and the Transform Fill option from the Drawing toolbar

2 Select the object whose gradient you want to edit

3 Click and drag the centre point to change the position of the gradient

Changing a gradient's shape

| Select the Paint Bucket tool and the Transform Fill modifier as on the previous page and select the object to be edited

Three small buttons appear around a gradient fill when it is selected. These are on the right hand side of the object and are, from top to bottom:

- *Change Gradient Shape*
- *Change Gradient Radius, and;*
- *Change Gradient Rotation*

2 Click and drag on the Change Gradient Shape button to make the gradient larger or smaller

Changing a gradient's radius

| Select the Paint Bucket tool and the Transform Fill modifier as above and select the object to be edited

2 Click and drag on the Change Gradient Radius button to make the gradient's radius larger or smaller

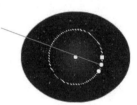

Applying rotation to a gradient has no effect unless its centre has already been moved, as on the previous page, or its shape has been changed.

Changing a gradient's rotation

| Select the Paint Bucket tool and the Transform Fill modifier as above and select the object to be edited

2 Click and drag on the Change Gradient Rotation button to rotate the gradient

More colour options

Swapping colours

It is possible to swap the selected colours for the stroke and the fill options. To do this:

1 Click here on the Drawing toolbar

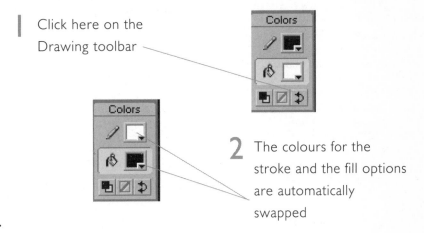

2 The colours for the stroke and the fill options are automatically swapped

To access the Mixer panel, select Window> Panels>Mixer from the Menu bar.

Using the Mixer panel

Instead of having to use two separate routes each time you want to change the colour for the stroke and the fill options, they can both be changed at the same time using the Mixer panel:

Select either the line colour option or the fill colour option and then select a colour for each one

Click here to make the selected colours black and white

Selecting the colours for the stroke colour or the fill colour can be done in the same way as shown on page 72, once the relevant option has been chosen.

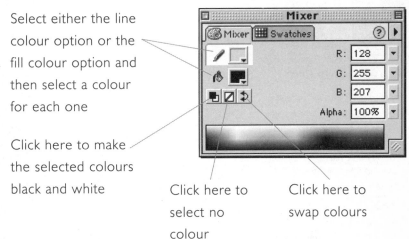

Click here to select no colour

Click here to swap colours

Selecting colours

Solid colours can be selected with the Arrow tool or the Lasso tool. However, this is not always effective if you want to select areas of colour within a bitmap image i.e. a photograph. To do this, the Lasso tool can be used in conjunction with its Magic Wand modifier:

1 Import an image and break it apart so that individual areas of colour can be selected (see the DON'T FORGET tip)

2 Select the Lasso tool and the Magic Wand modifier

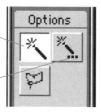

3 Select the Magic Wand Settings modifier and enter the relevant settings

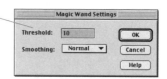

4 Select an area of colour on the bitmap by clicking on it once with the Magic Wand tool

Adding text

In Flash, text can be more than just plain words on the screen. It can serve this purpose perfectly well, but it can also be used to create animations. These will be dealt with in Chapter Nine. However, it is important to look at the basics of text entry. Two points to remember:

- Text is created as an overlay level object, so it is placed on top of any stage level objects on the Stage

- In its original format text is created in text labels or boxes. These can be edited and formatted in a similar way to text in a word processing program. However, text can also be broken apart so that individual words and letters can be used as shapes and formatted accordingly

Text can be added as text labels or text boxes.

To add a text label

Select the Text tool in the Character panel, then select the following as appropriate:

The text options can also be selected from the Menu bar. Select Text and then either Font, Size, Style, Align or Tracking.

To access the Character panel, select Window> Panels> Character from the Menu bar.

In the Character panel there is a check box for kerning. This sets the amount of space between individual letters.

Click here to select a font

Click here to select a font size

Click here to select tracking and character position

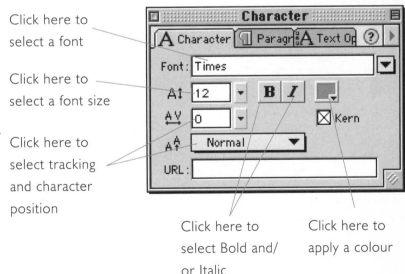

Click here to select Bold and/ or Italic

Click here to apply a colour

Text labels can be used to position specific words at the end of a line. Press Return after the required word, and a new line will be started underneath it.

2 Click on the Stage with the Text tool. Enter the text into the text label

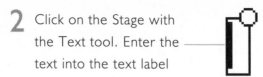

3 The text will continue along the Stage, and

A text label will keep expanding

eventually off the edge into the Work Area, unless Return is pressed to create a new line

To add a text box

1 Follow Step 1 on page 79

A text label is denoted by a small circle in the top right hand corner of the box into which the text is typed. A text box is denoted by a small square.

2 Click and drag the text crosshair on the Stage to create a text box of a specific width

3 When the text is entered it will wrap (move to the next line down) when it exceeds the width of the text box. The text will expand downwards, increasing the height of the text box, but the width will remain constant

Text in a text box will wrap downwards, expanding the box.

Formatting text

General formatting

Text can be aligned in either a text label or a text box by inserting the cursor within a paragraph and selecting the Alignment options in the Paragraph panel (see below).

1 With the Text tool, select the text by clicking and dragging the cursor over it

2 Select options from the Character panel, as with creating text on page 79

3 The text displays the selected choices:

TEXT IS VERSATILE

Paragraph formatting

For paragraph properties, line spacing is always measured in a default of points. The margin and indent measurements default to the settings applied to the ruler. This can be changed by selecting Modify>Movie and entering a new unit of measurement in the Ruler Units box.

1 Select the Paragraph panel by selecting Window>Panels>Paragraph from the Menu bar

2 Enter settings in the Paragraph panel

Alignment options

The amount the left and right margins are indented

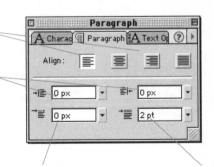

The amount the first line of each paragraph is indented

The amount of space between lines

Manipulating text

When rotating text, the greatest impact can be achieved by rotating individual words or letters. If too much text is rotated the effect is lost and it becomes difficult to read.

In addition to standard formatting for text, it can also be manipulated as if it were a graphic, rather than plain text.

Rotating and resizing

As with graphical objects, words or letters can be rotated and resized:

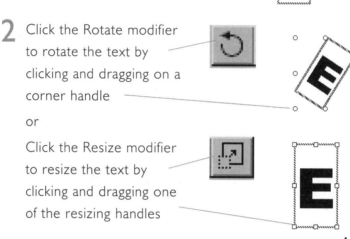

1 | With the Arrow tool select a word or letter by clicking on it once

2 | Click the Rotate modifier to rotate the text by clicking and dragging on a corner handle

or

Click the Resize modifier to resize the text by clicking and dragging one of the resizing handles

After text has been broken apart it may still be selected, which is denoted by shading over the affected area. Deselect the text by clicking anywhere away from it on the Stage. Then select the Arrow tool and move it over the text to reshape it. However, make sure not to select the object itself.

Reshaping text

Text can also be reshaped like a graphical object:

Reshaping objects is covered in Chapter Four, pages 62–63.

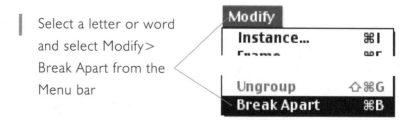

1 | Select a letter or word and select Modify > Break Apart from the Menu bar

2 | Click and drag either a corner point or a curve point to reshape the text

Symbols and instances

Flash has a function for creating an object once and then using it numerous times, without significantly increasing the size of the movie file. The two items used for this are called 'symbols' and 'instances'. A symbol is a master object which can be reused numerous times to create copies (instances) on the Stage. This chapter looks at creating and editing symbols and instances. It also looks at the Library, which is the area where symbols are stored.

Covers

Chapter Six

Symbols and instances defined

Whenever a symbol is created it is automatically placed in the Flash Library. This is an area for storing the items that are used in a particular movie – see pages 86–89.

Symbols and instances play a vital role in ensuring Flash's ability to create graphic-intensive movies, while still maintaining file sizes small enough to achieve an acceptably fast downloading time. Symbols are reusable items and they can consist of animations, static graphics, text or interactive buttons. An instance is created from a symbol and when it is placed on the Stage it appears identical to the symbol from which it was created. So an instance of a star graphic would look exactly like its symbol, at least when it is first placed on the Stage.

However, although instances look as if they are straight copies of the original symbols they are in fact only *references* to the symbol. This means they are not actually objects in their own right and so take up virtually no file space. So, a dozen instances could be created from one symbol and the amount of file space taken up would be only a little more than that occupied by the original symbol. This is invaluable if you want to use the same object numerous times in a movie. In addition, instances do not have to look exactly like the symbol from which they were created: it is possible to change their size and colour to give the effect of several different objects, while still referring them back to one original symbol.

Although individual instances can be edited independently of the original symbol and any other instances created from it, if the symbol is edited these changes will affect all of the instances of it on the Stage.

Six instances created from one symbol. Each instance has been edited by either recolouring, resizing or

rotating but they all still refer back to the original symbol

Types of symbols

There are three types of symbol, each of which can be used for certain functions. In addition, there are two other items that act in a similar way to symbols, even though they do not technically fall into this category:

Symbol types are also known as behaviours i.e. how the symbol reacts when it is placed in a movie.

- *Graphics.* These are the objects that are created with the Flash drawing tools. Not all graphics have to be turned into symbols and if it is an item that is only going to be used once, and remain static throughout the movie, then there is little point in changing it into a symbol. However, if a graphic is going to be reused throughout a movie, or even used in another movie, then it is worth turning it into a symbol. This operation is very quick and can save a lot of time and effort

Symbols have their own timelines that run independently of a movie's main Timeline. This is particularly important for button and movie clip instances since it gives them greater flexibility in the way they relate to the main movie i.e. a movie clip could be playing even though the main Timeline has stopped.

- *Buttons.* These are interactive objects that perform an action when they are pressed by the user. They can be programmed to perform a number of actions and these are looked at in detail in Chapter Ten

- *Movie clips.* These are animations that are placed within a movie. They are self-contained animated objects which can be used multiple times in a movie. Movie clips are a powerful and flexible way to create impressive animated effects and they are looked at in detail in Chapter Nine

- *Bitmaps and sounds.* Several types of bitmap images and sounds can be imported into Flash. They are then treated like symbols and the equivalent of instances can be created from them

Once symbols have been created they are placed in the Library. Before looking at how to create symbols it will be useful to look at the function of the Library and how it deals with symbols. This is covered on the following pages.

The Library

The Library is the storage area where the content of a Flash movie is contained. All of the elements of a movie can be kept here and symbols are placed here automatically when they are created. They are then dragged from the Library onto the Stage to create instances.

Accessing the Library

1 If the Library is not already showing, select Window>Library from the Menu bar

2 Select an item and it will be displayed in the Preview window. The items in the Library are displayed here with an icon depicting their type

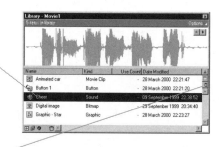

3 Click here to expand the Library window. This gives fuller details about each item stored in the Library

Click here to return to the standard Library window

When you first start creating a Flash movie you may think it is unnecessary to create numerous folders. However, the number of items you want to store in the Library will soon increase and folders are a good way to organise them.

If new folders are created in the main Library window these are known as root folders. These could be used for items entitled 'animations', 'buttons' and 'graphics'.

Folders can also be created inside other folders and these are known as sub-folders. These are created by double-clicking on an existing folder and creating a new folder as normal.

Creating new folders

One of the main functions of the Library is as a management system for all of the reusable items in a movie. In this respect it is similar to a file management system such as Windows Explorer in Windows or Finder on the Mac. As with these, it is possible to create folders and sub-folders for storing items. To create a folder:

1 At the point where you want to insert a new folder click here on the Library window

2 The folder name will be highlighted as 'untitled folder 1'. Type a new name for the folder

Deleting items

All objects within the Library can be deleted, including entire folders:

1 Select the item to be deleted and click here on the Library window

2 A warning dialog box appears to check that you really want to delete this item. Click Delete

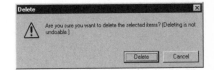

The Library menu

Some of the functions of the Library, such as creating new folders and deleting items, can be accessed from icons within the Library. Other functions are accessed from the Library Options menu:

Click here to access the Library Options menu

Click here to sort items in the Library. This can be done by Name, Kind, Use Count (the number of times an item has been used in a movie), or Date Modified, depending on which heading is selected. Maximise the Library window to view all of the column headers.

Items in the Library can be moved from one folder to another by dragging and dropping. Select the item you want to move. Click and drag it until it is over the folder into which you want to put it and release.

The functions on the Library Options menu are:

- *New Symbol.* This creates a new symbol. (Symbol creation is covered on pages 90-93)

- *New Folder.* The same as using the new folder icon

- *Rename.* Enables the selected item to be renamed

- *Move to New Folder.* Creates a new folder and moves the selected item into it

- *Duplicate.* Makes a copy of the selected item. This can be useful if you want to change a symbol's properties i.e. change a graphic into a button, but still maintain the same appearance for the item

- *Delete.* The same as using the Delete icon

...cont'd

If you have a Library collection from one movie and you want to use some of the items in another you can make them available.

Select File>Open as Library and the Open as Library dialog box will display all of the movies that have already been created. Select one then Open. This movie's Library will become available in the current movie and all of its contents can be used.

In Flash 5 it is also possible to create shared Libraries, where items can be shared across numerous movies. This is useful for individuals and also teams working on one project.

To create a shared Library, select an item in the Library and set its linkage properties using the Linkage button from the Library options. When the current movie is saved, a shared Library is saved at the same time.

To access a shared Library, select File>Open As Shared Library from the Menu bar and select the library you want to use. The items in it will then be available in the current movie. However, it is not possible to edit the symbols in a shared Library, without removing their shared properties.

- *Edit*. Enables a symbol's properties to be edited

- *Edit with*. This enables you to edit bitmap images in an external image editing program, such as Fireworks

- *Properties*. Displays the selected item's properties i.e. its name and its behavior

- *Linkage*. This is used to share elements of the current Library across numerous movies

- *Define Clip Parameters*. This can be used to add values to existing symbols

- *Select Unused Items*. Selects all of the items that have not been used in the movie

- *Update*. This updates any editing changes that have been made to an imported item

- *Play*. This plays sounds, movie clips or buttons

- *Expand Folder*. By double-clicking, this expands the selected folder to view all of its contents

- *Collapse Folder*. This collapses the selected open folder so none of the items in it are visible

- *Expand All Folders*. This expands all of the folders in the Library

- *Collapse All Folders*. This collapses all of the folders in the Library

- *Keep Use Counts Updated*. This automatically updates the counter for the number of times each item in the Library has been used.

- *Shared Library Properties*. This displays the properties of any shared Libraries

- *Update Use Counts Now*. This updates the use counter if Keep Use Counts Updated unchecked

Creating symbols – the conversion route

Symbols can be created by two methods:

- Converting existing items into symbols

Frames are looked at in greater detail in Chapter Eight.

- Creating symbols from scratch (this is done in Symbol Editing Mode) and then adding content

All three types of symbols (graphics, buttons and movie clips) can be created using either method but the preferred option is different depending on the type of symbol being created:

Buttons and movie clips are created in Symbol Editing Mode. This has all of the same facilities as for creating items on the main Stage. Once the symbol editing process has been completed the item (along with its own timeline and frames) can be placed on the main Stage.

- Since graphic symbols do not require any animation or interactivity they do not have to be edited beyond their initial state i.e. a single frame. Therefore they can be converted directly into symbols

- Buttons and movie clips both require more than one frame's worth of content and so it is best to create a blank symbol and then add all of the content from scratch

Converting objects into symbols

1. Select the required objects on the main Stage. These can be stage level objects, overlay level object, text, groups or other symbols

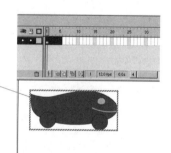

2. Select Insert > Convert to Symbol from the Menu bar

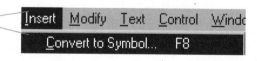

If you do not give symbols names when they are created you will end up with several similarly named items, which could become confusing.

3 Type a name for the symbol. The default will be something like Symbol 7 (or the next sequential number for the symbols that have been created)

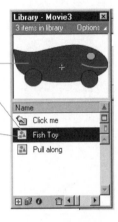

4 Select the type of symbol to be created (its behaviour). Select OK

5 The symbol is placed in the Library and displayed in the Preview window

An instance can also be created from the Library by clicking and dragging the symbol's name onto the Stage.

If an instance is deleted from the Stage it will not affect the symbol in the Library. However, if a symbol is deleted from the Library, all instances of it on the Stage will also be deleted.

6 Click and drag the symbol to create an instance of it on the Stage

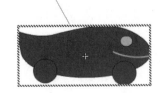

Creating a new symbol

For button or movie clip symbols it is best to create them from scratch using the New Symbol function. They can be created by converting an item into a symbol and then adding any additional elements that are required for the interactive button or the animation. However, since it can become slightly complicated as to what is a symbol and what is an item on the main Stage, it is probably best to stick to this method for buttons and movie clips.

Graphics can also be created from scratch using this method.

There are three ways to begin creating a new symbol from scratch:

Select Insert>New Symbol

or

Access the Library Options menu by clicking here, and selecting New Symbol

or

Click the New Symbol icon in the Library

When a new symbol is created it is automatically placed in the Library once OK is selected in the Symbol Properties box. The content of the symbol can then be added, or it can be added (or edited) at any time in the future. See page 95 for more information about editing symbols.

Each method accesses the Symbol Properties dialog box. Enter a name and select a behaviour for the symbol you want to create. Select OK

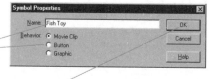

Creating button symbols involves creating four different states for the button:

* *one for before it has been activated (Up)*
* *one for when the mouse cursor passes over it (Over),*
* *one for when it is clicked on (Down), and;*
* *one for the area around the button that can activate its functions (Hit).*

Button symbols are looked at in more detail in Chapter Ten.

3 Symbol Editing Mode is then accessed. This is the environment in which the symbol will be created. This is the Symbol Editing Mode for creating a button

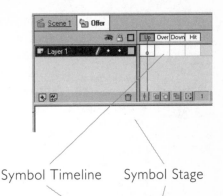

Symbol Timeline   Symbol Stage

This is the environment for creating a movie clip. It looks the same as the main Stage environment, but it is actually the movie clip symbol's own individual stage and timeline

Movie clip symbols can be used independently on the main Stage. However, they can also be inserted into graphics, button symbols and even other animations. Movie clips are looked at in more detail in Chapter Nine.

4 The symbol is added to the Library as soon as it has been created, even if no content has been added at this point

Symbol Editing Mode

Since new symbols are created with their own stage and timeline it can sometimes become confusing as to whether you are working on the main Stage or in Symbol Editing Mode. However, it is possible to identify in which mode you are working and switch between the two:

You have to double-click on the symbol icon in the Library and not the symbol name to access Symbol Editing Mode. If you double-click on the name this will just highlight it, so that its name can be changed by overtyping.

1 To open a symbol in Symbol Editing Mode, double-click on the symbol icon in the Library

or

Click here at the right-hand side of the toolbar to access a list of the symbols in the movie. Select one from the drop down list

Scenes can be used to divide a movie up into manageable chunks, which is particularly useful if you are working with very large movies. Scenes are looked at in more detail in Chapter Nine.

2 The name of the active symbol is displayed here. This denotes you are working in Symbol Editing Mode

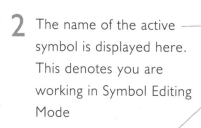

3 Click on the scene name to return to the main Stage

or

Click here and select a scene to move to

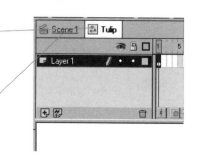

Editing symbols

Once changes have been applied to a symbol these will be applied to all instances of the symbol that have already been placed on the Stage. So if a circle symbol is changed to a square, all of the circle instances will become squares too.

Once a symbol has been created it can still be edited to change both its properties and its appearance. Its appearance can be altered by editing it in Symbol Editing Mode. In addition to the methods in Step 1 on the facing page, Symbol Editing Mode can also be accessed as follows:

- Select an instance of the symbol on the Stage. Select Edit>Edit Symbols from the Menu bar

- Select an instance of the symbol on the Stage. Select Edit>Edit Selected from the Menu bar

- Select a symbol in the Library. Select Edit from the Library Options menu (click on the small arrow next to Options to access the menu)

The Instance panel displays information about the currently selected symbol and provides options for editing the corresponding symbol. To access the Instance panel, select Window>Panels>Instance from the Menu bar.

- Select a symbol in the Library and then double-click on the image in the Preview window

- Select a symbol on the Stage by clicking on it once. Then click on the Edit button in the Instance Panel

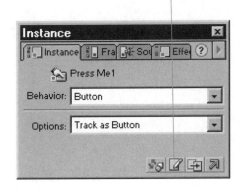

If you want to edit a symbol in its actual environment on the Stage, right-click (Windows) or Ctrl+click (Mac) on it and select Edit in Place from the contextual menu that appears. This allows you to edit the symbol while still viewing the relationship between it and the objects around it. The other objects are visible but greyed out while the editing takes place.

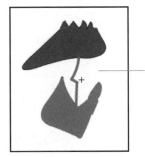

Once a symbol is in Editing Mode it can be modified in the same way as any other object. In this case a graphic symbol has been edited by reshaping with the Arrow tool

Duplicating symbols

When using symbols there may be occasions when you want to use the same item for a different purpose. For example, you could have a graphic that remains static throughout your movie, except for one part when you want to animate it for added impact. It is possible to create a graphic symbol and then go through the whole creation process again, only this time assigning a movie clip behaviour to the symbol and editing it accordingly. However, it is much quicker to create a duplicate of the original symbol and then edit its content. To do this:

1 Select a symbol in the Library and select Duplicate from the Library Options menu

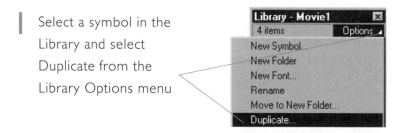

If a duplicate symbol is not assigned a name when it is created it is given the same name as the original but with 'copy' after it.

2 In the Symbol Properties dialog box, type a name for the duplicate symbol and select a behaviour. Select OK.

Using the Instance panel

Duplicate Symbols can also be created with the Instance panel:

Click here and then enter a name for the duplicate symbol in the Symbol Name dialog box

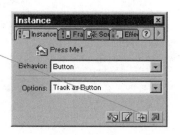

Editing instances

As shown on page 91, instances are created by selecting a symbol in the Library and dragging it onto the Stage. The object on the Stage is always an instance and the symbol itself never appears outside the Library (although it is possible to edit a symbol by accessing one of its instances on the Stage).

Individual instances can have their size, rotation and colour properties edited and this does not affect the symbol from which they were created, or other instances from the same symbol.

Resizing and rotating

If you want to create objects based on the same symbol but with different sizes and orientations this can be done by resizing and rotating individual instances:

1 With the Arrow tool, select an instance on the Stage

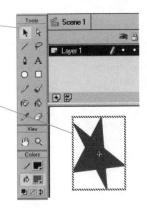

2 Select either the Rotate or the Scale option from the toolbar and rotate or resize using the handles that appear

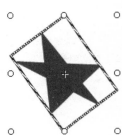

Editing colour properties

It is possible to edit an instance's colour in a number of ways: changing its brightness, tint, and transparency. To edit an instance's colour:

When instances are selected on the Stage their properties are displayed in the Instance panel.

1 Select an instance on the Stage by clicking on it once. Select the options from the Effects panel (if it is not showing, select Window>Panels>Effects from the Menu bar

2 In the Effects panel, click here to edit the brightness of the instance

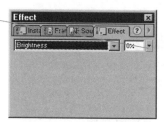

In the Tint dialog box, the Tint Amount option determines the level at which the selected colour is applied. If it is at 0% the original colour will be unaffected. If it is at 100% the selected colour will be applied in full.

Enter values here to edit the tint, i.e. create a new colour, or click here to select a colour

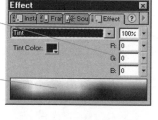

Click here to set the Alpha properties i.e. how opaque/transparent an object is

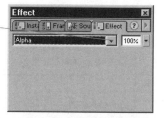

In the Alpha dialog box, 0% in the Alpha option makes an object completely transparent.

The Advanced settings enable you to select the colour properties and the alpha settings at the same time

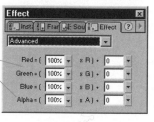

Bitmaps and sound

In addition to creating drawing objects within Flash it is also possible to import bitmap images, such as photographs, and sound files. This chapter looks at how to import and edit both of these items and shows how they can be used to enhance a Flash movie.

Covers

Chapter Seven

Using bitmaps

Hard copy images such as graphics or photographs can be converted into bitmaps by using a scanner. This creates a digital image which can then be imported into Flash, providing it is created in an acceptable format.

Images taken with a digital camera can also be imported into a Flash movie.

Bitmaps are images that are created by using pixels (tiny coloured dots) to represent the image. Although Flash uses a different method to create graphics (vector-based, using a mathematical formula) it can support certain bitmap formats and it is possible to incorporate them into a movie.

Using bitmap images has a number of advantages:

- More complex images such as photographs can be used

- Bitmaps can be used as stand-alone images or they can be incorporated into backgrounds or fills

- There is greater opportunity for creating eye-catching content

The main drawback of bitmaps is that they generally take up more disk space than vector-based graphics, which adds to the size of a Flash movie and so has an adverse effect on the all-important downloading time. However, there are techniques that can be used to compress the size of bitmaps when they are incorporated in Flash movies.

Types of bitmaps

There are dozens of different formats for bitmap images. The ones that are supported by Flash are:

It is also possible to import graphics from other vector-based programs such as Macromedia Freehand or Adobe Illustrator.

- BMP (Windows only)

- PICT (Mac only)

- JPEG (Windows and Mac)

- GIF (Windows and Mac)

- PNG (Windows and Mac)

Images in these formats can be imported into Flash and used in their original format. In addition to this, they can also be broken apart to allow for standard Flash image editing functions to be applied to them.

Importing bitmaps

Once a bitmap has been created it can be imported into a movie from your hard drive, from an external storage device such as a Zip drive, or from a digital source such as a digital camera or a scanner. To import a bitmap:

If you want to import a bitmap directly from an external device, select this location at the top of the Import dialog box and then select the bitmap.

1 Select File>Import from the Menu bar

2 Locate the bitmap you want to import. Select Open (Windows) or Add>Import (Mac)

When importing bitmaps, Flash will only display files whose format is supported by the program.

3 The bitmap is placed on the Stage and a copy is also placed in the Library. Although this is not strictly speaking a symbol, copies of the bitmap can be made by dragging it onto the Stage from the Library

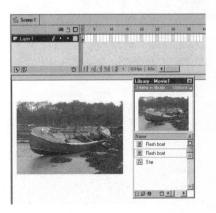

Bitmap properties

When a bitmap is imported into a movie one of the most important issues is its file size. This is determined by the images resolution i.e. the number of pixels in the image. The higher the resolution then the larger the file size. This is measured in dots per inch (dpi) and if you are creating bitmaps for use in a Flash movie it is best to set the dpi to a maximum of 72. This is because computer monitors generally cannot display more than 72 dpi, so anything of a higher quality will be wasted and just lead to an unnecessarily large file size.

When a bitmap has been imported into a movie it is possible to edit some of its properties so that it appears at the highest quality but with the smallest file size. To edit a bitmap's properties:

1 Double-click on a bitmap in the Library (or click on it once and select Properties from the Library Options menu)

2 Edit the settings in the Bitmap Properties dialog box:

Preview window

Allow smoothing – check this on to give the image a smoother appearance

Compression options – determines how an image is compressed, thereby decreasing its file size

Tracing bitmaps

It is possible to turn bitmaps into vector-based graphics by using a technique called tracing. This can give greater flexibility when it comes to editing the bitmap. To trace a bitmap:

Tracing bitmaps can be a hit and miss affair and it can take a few minutes for the vector image to be produced.

1 Place a copy of the bitmap on the Stage and select it

2 Select Modify>Trace Bitmap from the Menu bar

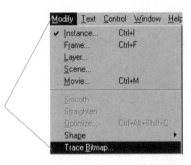

3 Enter values in the Trace Bitmap dialog box:

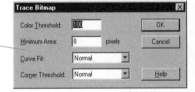

To get the best results when tracing photographs it is necessary to set:

- *a low colour threshold*
- *a small minimum area*
- *a tight, or very tight, curve fit, and;*
- *a normal corner fit*

However, this can greatly increase the file size of your movie.

- *Color Threshold.* This determines how much each pixel has to differ in colour from the one next to it for a new vector calculation to take place. A higher threshold means fewer calculations. The settings are between 1 and 200

- *Minimum Area.* This determines how many neighbouring pixels are included in calculating the colour. This can be between 1 and 1000

- *Curve Fit.* This determines how closely a vector image follows the original. The settings are: Pixels, Very Tight, Tight, Normal, Smooth and Very Smooth

- *Corner Fit.* This determines whether the vector image creates smooth or sharp corners. The settings are: Many corners, Normal and Few corners

Bitmaps as fills

Once a bitmap has been imported into a movie it can be used as an individual image or it can be used as a fill for objects, in the same way as solid colours and gradients. To use a bitmap as a fill:

Once a bitmap has been broken apart, it becomes a stage level object and takes on the appropriate properties.

1 Select a bitmap on the Stage. Select Modify>Break Apart from the Menu bar

The Lasso tool and Magic Wand options can be used to select colours within a broken apart bitmap.

With the relevant tools selected, click on an area of colour on the bitmap. Depending on the Magic Wand options, an area of colour will be selected, which can then be used as a fill. This technique is also covered on page 78.

2 The bitmap becomes shaded, indicating that it has been broken apart

3 Draw an object on the Stage that is going to be filled with the bitmap

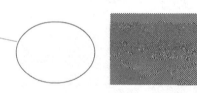

4 Select the Dropper tool from the Drawing toolbar and click once with it on the broken apart bitmap

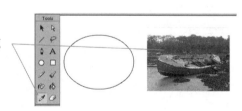

Once a bitmap fill has been chosen this becomes the default for all drawing objects, until another fill is selected.

5 The tool turns into the Paint Bucket. Click inside the drawing object to add the bitmap fill

Editing bitmap fills

A bitmap fill is created using an image with the same dimensions as the original bitmap. This is fine if the object to be filled is the same size as the bitmap. However, if it is smaller then only a small amount of the bitmap may appear and if it is larger the bitmap will be tiled i.e. the image will be repeated in a tile pattern. However, it is possible to edit bitmap fills once they have been applied to a drawing object:

Tiling can produce some interesting effects for both drawing objects and backgrounds. Experiment with different images to see how they appear when tiled.

1 Select the Paint Bucket tool and the Transform option. Click within the drawing object that contains the bitmap fill. The Fill Transform box appears around the bitmap that was clicked on

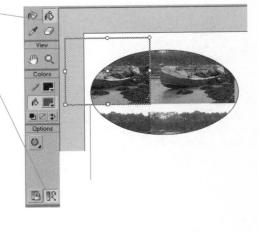

Make sure the bitmap-filled drawing object is deselected before you click on it with the Paint Bucket and Transform option.

2 Click and drag the centre point to move the position of the bitmap within the object

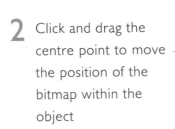

If a drawing object is too small for the bitmap fill, only one area will be visible in the object. The fill can be resized using the options on this page so it is all visible in the object. However, it may then be too small to be viewed properly.

3 Click and drag the horizontal and vertical resizing handles to make the fill larger or smaller

4 Click and drag the horizontal skew handle to skew the fill accordingly

5 Click and drag the vertical skew handle to skew the fill accordingly

The button at the bottom left corner of the Transform Fill box is the Proportional Resize button. This resizes the fill horizontally and vertically in equal proportions.

6 Click and drag the rotation handle to rotate the fill left or right

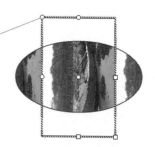

Using sound

Sound in Flash

In addition to its array of visual functions, Flash can also utilise sound files to give an extra dimension to a movie. These files have to be created outside Flash and then imported into a movie. They can then have some basic editing techniques applied to them. The three sound formats that can be used in Flash are:

Flash comes with a selection of its own prerecorded sounds. Select Libraries>Sounds from the Menu bar to access them. These libraries also contain buttons, graphics and movie clips.

- .WAV (Windows)

- .AIFF (Mac)

- MP3 (Windows and Mac)

There are two ways to use sounds in Flash:

Support for MP3 sound files is a new feature in Flash 5. MP3 has become one of the most popular file types for music on the Web and there are numerous sites where these can be downloaded. The most popular is:

- *http://www.mp3.com*

- *An event-driven sound.* These are sounds that play when a certain action is performed, such as an interactive button being pressed. Event-driven sounds have to be downloaded completely before they play and the sound plays in its entirety before stopping, regardless of what else is happening in the movie

- *Streamed sounds.* These are sounds that are synchronised with the content of the movie, such as a soundtrack for a specific piece of animation. Streamed sounds are downloaded as each piece is required so even if it is a long sound file the user will be able to start listening to it before the whole clip has downloaded

Most clip art collections on CD-ROMs also have libraries of sound clips.

Creating sounds

Sounds can be created using a simple sound recorder such as the ones that come with most Windows operating systems (Sound Recorder) and Mac (SoundSimple). There are also numerous CD-ROMs that have sound collections on them, or you could try the following Web sites:

- http://www.webplaces.com/html/sounds.htm

- http://www.wavcentral.com/

Importing sounds

Sound files cannot be created directly within Flash so they have to be imported from the hard drive or an external storage source. To import a sound:

1 Select File>Import from the Menu bar

2 Locate the required sound file and select Open (Add>Import on the Mac)

3 The sound is placed in the Library automatically. A digital representation of the sound is displayed in the Preview window

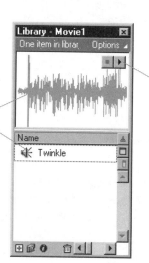

Click here to hear a selected sound

Editing sounds

A keyframe is inserted at any point in the movie when the content on the Stage changes.

Once sounds are in a movie, some simple editing techniques can be applied to them:

Changing the volume

1 Click once on the keyframe that contains the sound. The sound will be denoted by a straight line and its name will be displayed in the Sound panel

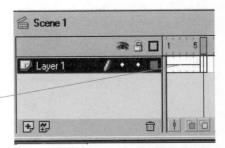

When working with sound files, create a new layer for each one. This will keep all of the sound files separate and make them easier to work with. For more information on layers, see Chapter Eight.

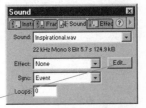

2 Click on Edit in the Sound panel. The sound file will be displayed. The top window is for the left channel of the sound and the bottom window is for the right channel

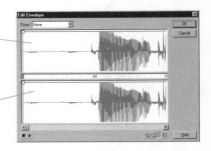

When editing the volume of a sound, increase or decrease it by the same amount for each channel. Otherwise, when the sound is played there will be different sound levels for the left and right speakers.

3 Click and drag here (the envelope handle) to move the line (the envelope line) to increase or decrease the sound accordingly

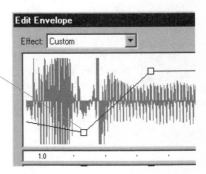

Fading sounds in

Fading in and out is a useful technique for introducing sounds subtly, rather than suddenly.

Select a sound on the Stage and click on Edit in the Sound panel (see the previous page). Drag the envelope handle to the base of the window. Click the envelope line to add a new handle and drag this to the top of the window. This will cause the sound to fade in

The time-in and time-out controls determine how much of a sound is cut off i.e. the whole of the sound is not played, just the portion between the two buttons.

Changing the start and end point

Click and drag here on the time-in button to make the sound begin at a different point. The same can also be done for the end point of the sound

The Effect options in the Edit Envelope dialog box are the same as those found on the Sound panel.

Sound effects and properties

Click here to apply special effects

Click here to zoom in or out

Click here to preview a sound and any effects that have been added.

Click here to view the sound timeline in frames or seconds

Frames and layers

Frames and layers are two important items for adding and controlling content in a movie. This chapter looks at inserting and editing frames and layers and how they can be used to simplify the editing process of a movie.

Covers

Chapter Eight

Working with frames

Frames are the components of a movie that allow content to be added on the Stage. They also play a vital role in creating animations. There are different types of frames but they all serve the same basic purpose: to control the way content is displayed and viewed in Flash.

Keyframes

The most significant type of frame is a keyframe. This is like a master frame that denotes there has been a change in the content on the Stage. Every movie has a blank keyframe pre-inserted, but this is blank until content is added to the Stage, when a solid bullet point is displayed on the Timeline.

The terminology of frames and keyframes comes from the days when all animations were drawn by hand.

The keyframes were the ones where a specific event occurred in the animation, such as a character turning its head, and the regular frames were the ones where there was only static content. These frames were known as in-between frames i.e. the frames in-between where the actual animation took place. This is where Flash takes one of its main animation terms from – tweening. This is the technique for adding frames in between two keyframes in an animation.

(Tweening is looked at in Chapter Nine.)

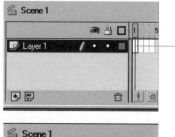

An empty keyframe, i.e. one with no content added on the Stage, is denoted by a blank frame

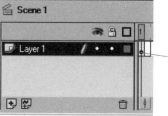

Once content has been added to the Stage, a solid circle appears in the keyframe

Frames can also have actions added to them (such as 'stop playing the movie' or 'move to a particular frame'). A keyframe that has had an action added to it is denoted with a small 'a' above the keyframe circle:

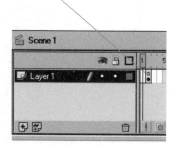

Actions can be added to keyframes to give them increased interactivity. See Chapter Ten for more on this

Once content has been added to a keyframe, this will remain visible on the Stage until another keyframe occurs:

To move between keyframes and regular frames click and drag on the Playhead.

If the content of a keyframe extends over more than one frame, this is known as a frame sequence. The end of this is denoted by a small rectangle on the timeline. This indicates that the content on the Stage will change after this. In Flash 5 it is possible to have empty frames between a frame sequence and the next keyframe.

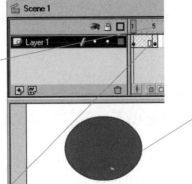

The content in the keyframe of frame 1 on the Timeline is a circle. Since another keyframe does not occur until frame 5, the circle will remain on the Stage until that point.

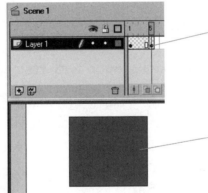

The content in the keyframe of frame 5 on the Timeline is a square. At this point, the circle that appears in the first four frames will disappear and the square will replace it

Keyframes are placed within the blank frames on the Timeline.

The speed at which frames are played in a movie (the frame rate) can be set by selecting Modify> Movie from the Menu bar and then entering a value in the Frame Rate box in the Frame Properties dialog box. The default is 12 frames per second, which is considered best for display on the Web.

Some points to remember about keyframes:

- Keyframes have to be added if you want to create animations or include interactivity

- All movies have to have at least one keyframe

- All movies begin with a blank keyframe already inserted in frame 1 of the Timeline

Regular frames

Regular frames contain the content of the nearest preceding keyframe and they can be used to determine the distance between keyframes and also the overall length of a movie. Regular keyframes are denoted by solid shading on the Timeline:

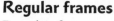

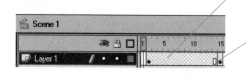

The end of a frame sequence is denoted by a hollow rectangle

Setting movie length with frames

A movie will not play beyond the last frame on the Timeline, whether it is a regular frame or a keyframe. In this way it is possible to set the length, in frames, of a movie. If you want a movie that is 20 frames long, then insert a regular frame or a keyframe at that point. (See the facing page for details on adding frames.)

Creating a background with frames

The background to a movie is a static element that can remain in place for the whole movie, allowing other objects to be placed on top of it.

1 Create your background in the keyframe in frame 1

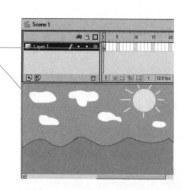

2 Insert a regular frame at the point where the movie will end. The background will occupy all of these frames

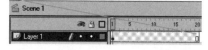

Adding frames

Regular frames and keyframes can be added at any point within a movie.

Adding regular frames

| Select a blank frame on the Timeline where you want the new frame added

A regular frame can be added within a group of existing regular frames.

Drag the playhead to the point where you want to add the frame, then do so as described on this page. This inserts a new regular frame to the right of the one that was selected. This can be done to extend the duration an item remains on the Stage during the movie. This increases the playing time of a movie.

To add more than one frame at a time, select the number of frames that you want to add, by clicking and dragging on the timeline, then select Insert>Frame from the Menu bar.

2 Select Insert>Frame from the Menu bar, or right-click (Windows), Ctrl+click (Mac), and select Insert Frame

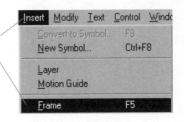

3 A regular frame is inserted and takes on the content of the nearest preceding keyframe

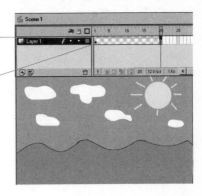

Adding keyframes

Keyframes should be added whenever you want to create a change in a movie. This could be a visual change, or the inclusion of an action that performs a certain task within the movie.

1 Select a frame on the Timeline where you want the new keyframe inserted

2 Select Insert>Keyframe (or Blank Keyframe) from the Menu bar, or right-click (Windows), Ctrl+click (Mac), and select Insert Keyframe (or Insert Blank Keyframe)

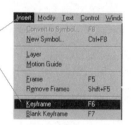

If you only want to make small changes between the content in successive keyframes, then the new keyframe option is the best one. If you want to make significant changes then it may be better to insert a blank keyframe and build the content from scratch.

3 A new keyframe has the same content as the preceding keyframe. This can be edited accordingly for the new keyframe

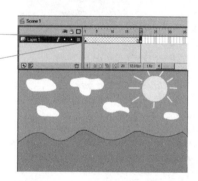

4 A new blank keyframe has no content, until items are added to the Stage in this keyframe

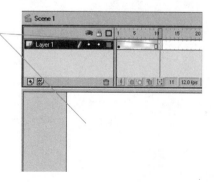

Deleting and copying frames

Deleting frames

Both regular frames and keyframes can be deleted from any point on the Timeline:

It is also possible to copy frames by selecting them and then dragging the selection to a new location. To do this, select the required frames by Alt+clicking (Windows) or Option+clicking (Mac) and then drag them to their new location. This will copy the frames and leave the original ones in place.

Select the regular frame or keyframe. Select Insert>Remove Frames or Insert> Clear Keyframe

Copying frames

Frames can be moved from one layer to another by selecting them and then dragging them between layers. They can also be copied between layers by selecting them and dragging them as described in the tip above.

1 Select a single frame by Ctrl+clicking on it on the Timeline, or select a range of frames by Ctrl+clicking on the first frame and then dragging over the range to be selected on the Timeline

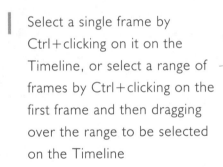

When a range of regular frames is copied, the preceding keyframe is also inserted at the point where the frames are pasted on the Timeline.

2 Select Edit>Copy Frames from the Menu bar

3 Select the frame where you want the copied frames to be placed. Select Edit>Paste Frames from the Menu bar

Frame properties

Various properties can be assigned to frames. These include those for animation (Tweening) and interactivity (Actions), which are looked at in Chapters Nine and Ten respectively. Sound files that are located in a particular frame can also be edited in the Frame Properties dialog box. A fourth option is for adding labels and comments to a frame. A label is an identifier that is used to locate specific frames within a movie when working with interactive elements. Comments can be added as reminders about the content of a frame. They do not affect the published movie and are for information only in the editing environment. To add labels and comments:

Labels and comments can be added to regular frames and keyframes, but if they are added to regular frames they always appear at the nearest preceding keyframe.

Comments can be used as reminders to do certain things during the editing process. This could include a comment to add a particular item to a frame or to start an animation at a certain point.

Access the Frame panel by selecting Window> Panels>Frame from the Menu bar. Select a frame and click here to add a label or a comment

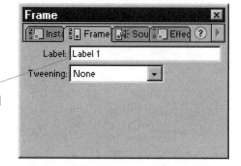

A label is denoted on the Timeline by a red flag and the name of the label

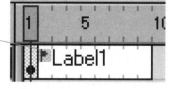

If the forward slashes are not inserted before the comment in the Frame panel, then it will appear as a label on the Timeline.

A comment is denoted on the Timeline by two green strokes and the name of the comment. These have to be inserted as forward slashes in the Frame panel when the comment is being added

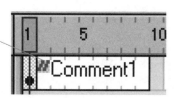

About layers

Layers are an organisation device in Flash that allows you to separate the content of a movie into manageable sizes. Layers act like sheets of glass placed one of top of another. Content can be added to each sheet and when they are compiled all of the content on the layers can be viewed together. Some points to remember about layers in Flash:

Use a new layer for each new element you add to the Stage.

- The order of layers is called the stacking order

- Content in the bottom layer that is covered by the next layer will not be visible, and so on through all of the layers

- It is possible to change the stacking order of layers

- When creating a new item (such as a drawing object, an animation, a bitmap, a sound or an interactive button) it is a good idea to place it on a new layer. This will make it easier to edit and it means you will not have any other items getting in the way

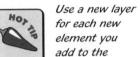

It is possible to hide the content of layers. This is useful if you want to work on a layer without being distracted by the content on other layers. See page 123 for details about hiding layers.

- Only one layer can be selected and worked on at a time

- The background of a movie should always be on a separate layer, at the bottom of the stacking order

- Layers can be given their own individual names

- Dozens of layers can be added to a single movie

- When a movie is published, Flash displays the content in frame 1 of all of the layers used. It then displays the content in frame 2 of all of the layers and so on

It is possible to lock layers so that the content cannot change by accident.

- Layers can have their own stacking order if they contain stage level and overlay level objects. This internal stacking order is preserved if the layer is moved within the overall stacking order

Working with layers

The order in which objects appear in a movie can be changed by altering the position of its layers.

The layers of a movie are displayed here.
The top layer (triangle) is the one that appears as the foremost on the Stage. If it covers other objects, or parts of objects, behind it then these items will not appear. Similarly the second layer (square) covers some of the object in the third layer and this is not visible

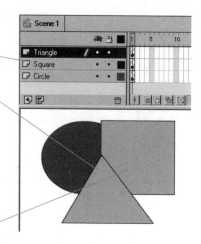

Click and drag a layer to move its position in the stacking order. This changes the relationship between the objects on the Stage. In this case the Circle layer has been moved to the top, so the circle moves to the front on the Stage and covers the items behind it

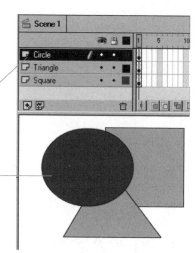

Inserting layers

All new movies are opened with one layer (entitled Layer 1), a Timeline and a blank keyframe in frame 1. Additional layers can be added at any time during the editing process and they also have a blank keyframe in frame 1. New layers can be inserted at any point in the stacking order of existing layers. To insert new layers:

If you select an item on the Stage that is on a different layer from the one currently being edited, the layer of the selected object will become the active one. This way, you can move between layers by clicking on different items on the Stage.

1 Select the layer above which you want to insert the new layer

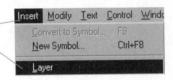

2 Click here to add a new layer or select Insert>Layer from the Menu bar

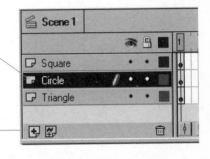

A layer can be renamed at any time, by double-clicking on its name and overtyping.

3 To rename the new layer, double-click on its name and overtype a new one

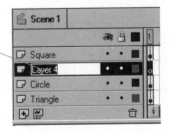

Layers do not add to the size of a movie. The content is the thing that adds to the file size, so you can use as many separate layers as you like.

4 Enter content for the new layer. This will appear on the Stage according to the layer's position in the stacking order

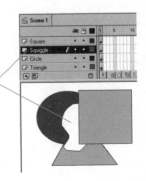

Deleting and copying layers

Deleting layers

If you decide you do not want to use the contents of a layer, it can be deleted from the movie:

If you delete a layer and its contents by mistake, select Edit>Undo

from the Menu bar immediately after you have performed the delete operation. The Undo function in Flash only applies to the immediately preceding editing action.

1 Select the layer to be deleted. Click the Wastebasket icon to remove it

2 The layer is removed from the stacking order and its contents are deleted from the Stage

Copying layers

If you want to use the same, or similar, content from one layer, this can be copied and pasted into a new layer. This is done with the Copy Frames and Paste Frames commands as shown on page 117:

1 Insert a new layer in the stacking order

2 Select all of the frames in the layer to be copied and then copy and paste them into the new layer. The new layer retains its original name but it now contains content

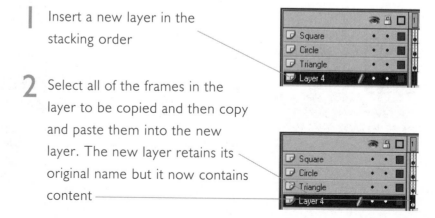

Layer modes

Only one layer can be the currently selected one. However, any layer can be placed in Hidden, Locked or Outline mode and it does not have to be selected first.

Layers have four modes that can be selected, to make it easier when working with multiple layers:

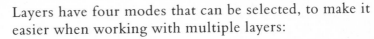

Current Mode. This is the active layer on the Stage and is denoted by a pencil icon next to the layer name

Locking layers is a good way to ensure the content is not edited by mistake.

Hidden Mode. This hides the contents of the selected layer and is denoted by a red cross in the column below the eye

Locked Mode. This locks the contents of the selected layer so it cannot be edited and is denoted by a padlock in the column below the padlock icon

Outline mode allows you to see the outlines of all of the layers on the Stage and can be a useful way of viewing how different objects overlap on different layers.

Outline Mode. This displays the contents of the selected layer as outlines only and is denoted by a coloured square in the column below the square

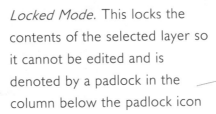

The colours for Outline mode can be changed by selecting Modify>Layer from the Menu bar and then selecting the required colour in the Outline Color box.

Individual layers can have Hidden, Locked or Outline modes applied to them. Also, all layers in a movie can have these modes applied by clicking on the icons at the top of the columns

Layer properties

Various attributes within a layer can be determined in the Layer Properties dialog box:

The Layer Properties dialog box can also be accessed by right-clicking (Windows) – or Ctrl+clicking (Mac) – on a layer and selecting Properties from the contextual menu that appears.

1 Select a layer and select Modify>Layer from the Menu bar

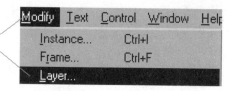

2 Select options for the layer's properties:

Double-click here and overtype to change the layer name

Click here to make the layer content visible or locked

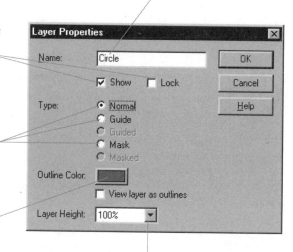

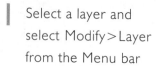

In addition to normal layers there are also Guide and Mask layers. Guide layers are used to help control an animation's movement (see Chapter Nine). Mask layers are used to hide certain parts of other layers (see the facing page).

Click here to select the type of layer (see the HOT TIP)

Click here to choose a colour if the layer is displayed in Outline mode

Click here to determine the height of the layer. The default is 100% but it can be changed to 200% or 300%, useful for viewing sound files in a layer

Mask layers

Mask layers are a special type of layer that works in a similar way to a stencil. A Mask layer can have objects added to it and it is then placed on top of another, regular layer. The content of the regular layer will only be visible through the content of the Mask layer: the rest of it masks the regular layer and hides any other objects. There are two important points to remember about Mask layers:

Once the concept of Mask layers is fully understood they can be used to create some highly artistic effects. It is an area that is worth persevering with and experimenting with.

- Regular layers have to be linked to Mask layers for the mask to function

- The content of the regular layer will only be visible through the area on the Mask layer that has content. Although the mask content may look as though it is covering the regular layer, the reverse is true. The content on the Mask layer acts like a window, allowing the content behind it to be visible

Creating a Mask layer

When adding content to the layer that is going to be the Mask layer (in this case the layer in Step 2) it does not matter about its colour. This is because when it is acting as a mask the objects will be completely transparent to allow the content below it to show through.

1 Create a regular layer and add content

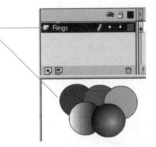

2 Add a new layer above the first layer and add content. Make sure it covers some of the content in the first layer

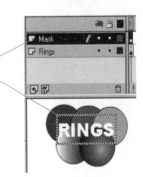

A Mask layer can be linked to several regular layers.

Mask layers are always above any regular layers which are linked to them. To link a regular layer to a Mask layer, click and drag the regular layer until the shaded line connected with the regular layer is directly below the Mask layer. Release and the regular layer becomes linked to the mask one.

To unlink a layer, click and drag it away from the Mask layer.

A Mask layer is denoted by a circle with a down pointing arrow inside it and a linked layer is denoted by a circle with a right pointing arrow

3 Select the layer that will be the Mask layer

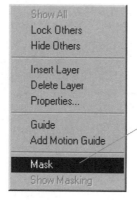

4 Right-click (Windows) or Ctrl+click (Mac) and select Mask

5 The Mask layer is now linked to the regular layer below. On the Stage the content on the regular layer is only visible through the content on the Mask layer

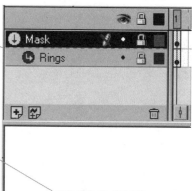

RINGS

Animation

This chapter looks at the animation techniques that can be used in Flash. It shows frame-by-frame animation and also how to move objects using motion tweening and how to change one shape into another using shape tweening. It also looks at animating text and creating movie clips.

Covers

Chapter Nine

Animation basics

Animation in Flash is, in many respects, just a technologically advanced version of traditional hand-drawn animation. In the days before computers, animations were created by drawing thousands of pictures and then playing them in sequence to create the animated effect. To reproduce the impression of movement, numerous drawings of an object were made, with each one slightly different from the preceding one. In this way the animators were able to create moving objects and characters using the same basic images.

In addition to creating moving objects, some items in an animation are static, such as the background. This difference helped form the hierarchy between the animation artists: the more highly paid and experienced ones created the moving items in an animation and the less well paid or less experienced artists usually stuck to the less technical drawings. This meant that there were groups of artists working on different layers within the same scene of animation. When all of the layers were collated, the final animation appeared.

In many respects Flash uses the same techniques as hand-drawn animations: objects can be animated on one layer, while other layers can contain elements that remain static throughout the movie. There are two types of animation that can be performed in Flash:

- *Frame-by-frame animation.* This is a form of animation where an object's appearance or position is changed slightly from frame to frame to create the impression of movement. This involves using a new keyframe for each change and it can be a time-consuming process

- *Tweened animation.* This is where you select the starting and finishing points for an object and Flash animates it by filling in all the frames in between (hence the name). Motion tweening (moving objects) and shape tweening (changing the shape of objects) can both be applied

Elements of animation

The Timeline

The Timeline is the collection of layers and frames that contain the content of a movie. It can also be used to control how objects are animated. The default Timeline shows the layers, frames and keyframes in the movie. However, this can be amended to show the information in other formats:

1 Click here to change the way frames are displayed on the Timeline

The Short option shrinks layers vertically. Use this if you want more layers to be visible at a time.

2 Choose a setting for how the frames are displayed

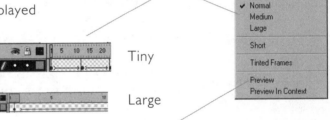

Tiny

If Tinted Frames is checked on then all regular frames and keyframes will be tinted.

Large

3 Click Preview to see the objects in each frame on the Timeline

Preview in Context shows the content for each frame but in the context of its actual size on the Stage.

Timeline status bar

At the bottom of the Timeline is a status bar that contains important information about the movie:

Current frame being viewed

Time elapsed to reach current frame (in seconds)

Fps during playback

The Playhead

The Playhead can be used to move between frames to view their contents. When the Playhead is positioned over a frame, all of the content at that point is displayed:

Click and drag the Playhead to move through a movie. If this is done

reasonably slowly it will display the results of any frame-by-frame animations, as the Playhead displays the contents of each frame in turn

Onion skinning

When creating an animation it can be a great help to see what the objects in the preceding and succeeding frames look like. This way it is possible to make any subtle amendments to the item you are working on so it will fit in smoothly with those around it. This is known as onion skinning and can be used as follows:

1 Create an animation. In this example it is a simple motion tween of a ball moving across the Stage

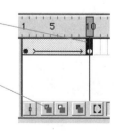

2 Select a frame in the animation. Click here to activate onion skinning

3 The object in the selected frame and the two before and after it are displayed

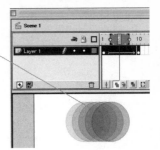

Content on locked or hidden layers is not affected by onion skinning.

4 Click and drag here to extend the number of frames that are included in the onion skinning

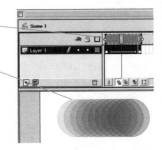

The Always Show Markers option on the Modify Onion Markers menu determines that the onion skin markers are always visible on the Timeline even if onion skinning is not activated. Anchor Onion keeps the markers locked, rather than moving with the Playhead, as they do by default.

5 Click here to view the onion skinning in outline format

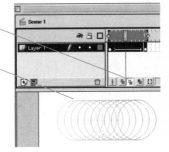

6 Click here to access the Modify Onion Markers menu. The bottom three options determine how many frames are affected by the onion skinning

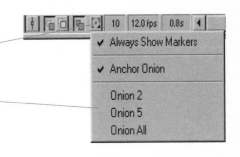

Scenes

Scenes in Flash are similar to their namesakes in a play: they are created separately but they are an important sequential part of the overall production. Scenes can be used to break up long movies into more manageable sizes, with different parts of the movie being broken up into separate scenes. For instance, if you have a movie that begins in an external location and then moves to an internal one, this could be broken up into two scenes. When using scenes it is worth remembering a couple of points:

- When creating a new scene, there is no evidence of other scenes in the editing environment, so if there are elements that are required throughout the whole movie, these will have to be recreated in the new scene

- Scenes play sequentially in the order they are created. However, it is possible to rename and reorder scenes in movies

Adding a new scene

New scenes can be inserted from the Menu bar or the Scene panel:

1 Select Insert>Scene from the Menu bar

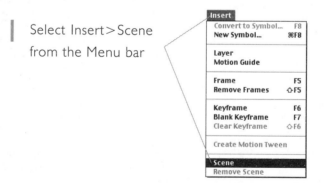

2 The name of the active scene is shown here

or:

Select Windows>Panels>Scene from the Menu bar to access the Scene panel

To delete a scene, select it in the Scene panel and click on the Delete button. This will remove the scene and all of its contents.

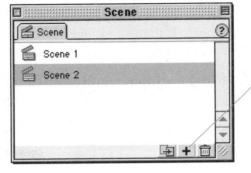

2 Click the Add button in the Scene panel to add a new scene

To reorder the sequence in which scenes play in a movie, click and drag on a scene in the Scene panel. Move it within the scene structure and then release. The movie will now play the scenes in this order.

Renaming a scene

Scenes can be given unique names, which makes it much easier when working with numerous scenes:

In the Scene panel, double-click on a scene

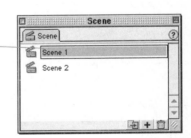

To move between scenes, access the Scene panel and select a scene. Also click on the Edit Scene icon at the right-hand side of the toolbar:

Click on the arrow to select a scene.

2 Type a new name for the scene in the Scene panel and press Enter or Return to apply the change

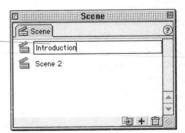

Frame-by-frame animation

A frame-by-frame animation involves inserting keyframes for each change in the animation and then editing the content accordingly. This way you are specifying the content for each frame of the animation: it is similar to drawing images on separate pages in a book and then flicking through it to create the animated effect. Frame-by-frame animations can be as simple or as complicated as you like, but the more complicated, then the longer it will take to edit the content for each frame.

Creating a simple frame-by-frame animation

To create an animation of a ball bouncing across the screen:

1 Open a new movie by selecting File>New. Create a background on the existing layer. Insert a regular frame at frame 20

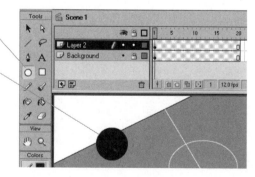

2 Insert a new layer above the background one and make sure the Playhead is at frame 1

3 At frame 1, select the Oval tool and draw a circle on the Stage (give it a fill colour but no outline; this will make it easier to work with)

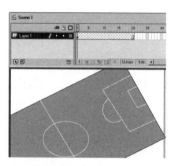

...cont'd

To make it easier to position objects when you are creating frame-by-frame animations, turn on the grid by selecting View>Grid from the Menu bar.

4 Select frame 5. Select Insert>Keyframe from the Menu bar. The ball will still be in the same position as it was in frame 1

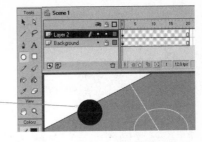

Once objects have been positioned in a keyframe it is possible to reposition them at any time in the editing process, by clicking on the relevant keyframe.

5 Click and drag the ball and move it to a new position on the screen

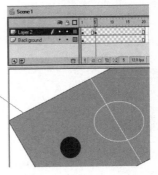

If you are creating complex animations such as people walking, draw each part separately i.e. the head, the body and the limbs. This is because in some keyframes certain parts may not move. Static elements, such as the body, can be reused, while the moving parts can be repositioned.

6 Insert new keyframes at frames 10, 15 and 20 and reposition the ball each time as in Step 5.

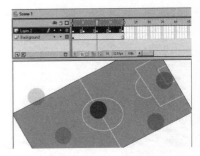

7 Select Control>Test Movie (or Test Scene) from the Menu bar to see the animation's progress. At this point it may look rather crude and jerky

To change the speed at which an animation plays (the frames per second speed) select Modify>Movie and change the value in the Frame Rate box. A higher value speeds up the animation and a lower figure slows it down. The Frame Rate box can also be accessed by double-clicking on the Frames Per Second (fps) box on the Timeline:

12.0 fps

With this example the animation will keep playing indefinitely in its current state. In order to stop it once the ball reaches the end of its path, a stop action has to be inserted at frame 20. This is looked at in Chapter Ten.

8 To smooth out the animation, select the frames between the keyframes that have already been inserted i.e. 2–4, 6–9 etc. Insert a keyframe into each one and reposition the ball slightly each time. Click on the onion skinning button to see how the position of the ball in each keyframe relates to those around it

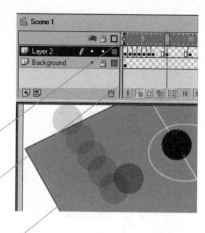

9 When all of the keyframes have been added and the ball repositioned, the path of the ball can be seen by stretching the onion skinning markers across the length of all of the frames used. Select Control>Test Movie (or Test Scene) to see the animation in action

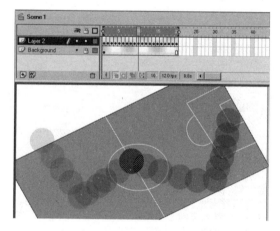

Motion tweening

Motion tweening is an animation technique that involves denoting the starting and ending point of an animation and then instructing Flash to fill in all of the frames in between. Only symbols, groups and text blocks can be used for motion tweens, but if a simple drawing object is required to be used in this way, Flash automatically converts it into a symbol. Motion tweens are excellent for depicting movement and a number of different properties can be defined, for additional creative power. To create a motion tween:

Motion tweening can create similar results to frame-by-frame animation, except it is usually quicker because Flash does a lot of the work for you. However, it does not allow for as much subtlety as a frame-by-frame effect.

Only symbols, groups or text blocks can be used in a motion tweening animation.

To insert a keyframe, select Insert> Keyframe from the Menu bar – alternatively, right-click (Windows) or Ctrl+click (Mac) – and select Insert Keyframe from the contextual menu.

1 Select File>New to open a new movie. In frame 1 add a drawing object. Convert it into either a graphic symbol or a group

2 Move to frame 20 on the Timeline. Insert a new keyframe and reposition the object

3 Select frame 1 again and select Insert>Create Motion Tween

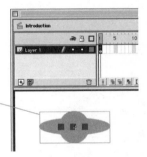

...cont'd

If you use the Playhead to view an animation this will not be at the same speed as when viewed in the testing environment or when it is published.

Turn on onion skinning to see how Flash has inserted the in-between frames for the animation.

4 An arrow now spans the frames between the two keyframes. This denotes that a tween has been created

5 View the animation by clicking here on the controller; dragging the Playhead from frame 1 to frame 20; or selecting Control>Test Movie (or Test Scene) from the Menu bar

6 If there is a broken, dotted line in the Timeline between the two keyframes, this means that the tween has not been created successfully. This could be because the object was not converted into a symbol or a group (it has to be in the same state in both keyframes) or if a blank keyframe was inserted instead of a regular keyframe

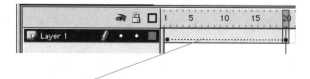

Editing a motion tween

Motion tweens can be edited so that the animation changes size, rotation and colour during the course of the tween. To apply editing techniques:

If these editing changes were applied to the motion tween in the example, it would begin small and transparent and then fade into view, increase in size and rotate 90 degrees. Effects like these can be used to give motion tweens a lot more versatility.

1 Select frame 1 and select the object with the Arrow tool. Select the Resize option from the Drawing toolbar. Resize the object by clicking and dragging one of the resizing handles

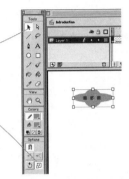

2 Select Window>Panels> Effect from the Menu bar and select the Alpha effect. Drag the slider to the bottom so that the Alpha setting is 0%. This will make the object completely transparent to start with and it will then fade in

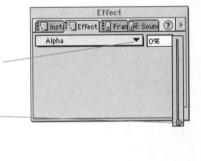

Using the Alpha effect to make objects transparent is a popular technique for making graphics and text fade in and out of a movie.

3 Select frame 20. Select the object with the Arrow tool and select the Rotate option. Rotate the object by clicking and dragging on the rotation handles

Motion guides

In a basic motion tween, the object moves in a straight line between the starting and ending keyframes. In addition to this, it is also possible to create a freehand path for the object to follow as it moves between its starting and ending points. This is done with a device called a motion guide and it can be inserted as follows:

1 Select the layer containing the motion tween. Select Add Guide Layer

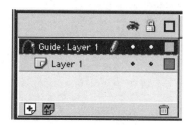

2 The Guide layer is inserted above the layer containing the motion tween (now linked to the Motion Guide layer)

3 Select the Pencil tool in the Drawing Toolbar and the Smooth option. Draw a freehand line joining the start and end points of the object

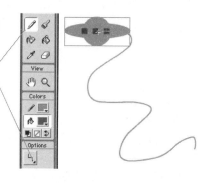

4 The motion tween will follow the path of the line

Motion guide orientation

It is possible to alter the way a motion tween moves along the motion guide path. This can have a significant effect, depending on the type of object being tweened.

The Easing slider can be used to change the speed at which a motion guided animation performs. Drag the slider down to make the animation start slowly and speed up. Drag the slider up to make the animation start quickly and slow down at the end.

I Click on the first frame of the linked layer (not the Guide layer) and Select Window>Panels>Frame from the Menu bar

2 The type of tween should be displayed here. Enter a value for Easing to determine how quickly or slowly you want the tween to begin. Check on the 'Orient to Path' box. This ensures the centre point of the object is rotated around the guide path

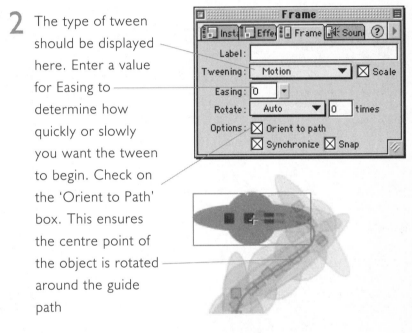

If the 'Snap' box is checked on, an object's centre point will snap to the motion path even if it is moved within its frame. If you want to move an object's centre point away from the motion path, check this box off.

3 Check off the 'Orient to path' box to keep the object parallel as it follows the guide path

Shape tweening

Shapes such as ovals and rectangles are excellent for shape tweening into letters or numbers.

The third type of animation that can be performed in Flash is shape tweening, or morphing. This is where one shape changes into another during the course of the animation e.g. turning a letter A into a number 2. This type of animation can only be done with simple shapes, broken apart text and stage level objects. Shape tweening cannot be applied to symbols, groups or bitmaps. To create a shape tween:

Shape tweening is an effective technique but it should not be overused in a movie, or else the impact will be diminished.

1 Select File>New to open a new movie. In frame 1 select the Text tool and access the Character panel. Type the letter A in a large font size (72 points or above)

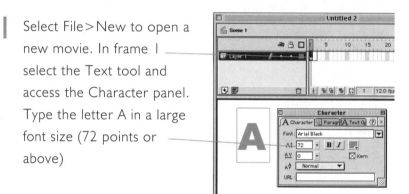

A blank keyframe is inserted in frame 20 because the content is completely different from the previous keyframe. If the content was the same but was going to appear in a different position (as in a motion tween) then a regular keyframe would have been inserted rather than a blank one.

2 Select the A on the Stage and select Modify>Break Apart from the Menu bar. This will turn the text into a format suitable for shape tweening

3 Select frame 20 and insert a blank keyframe (Insert>Blank Keyframe from the Menu bar). With the Text tool, type the number 2, the same size as the A in frame 1. Break it apart as above

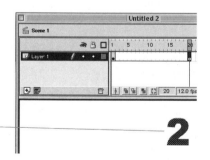

...cont'd

If you are using text for motion tweening and the tween does not work properly, make sure that both pieces of text are broken apart.

The Distributive and Angular options in the Tweening box determine how the tween operates. The Distributive option is better for curved objects; Angular is better for objects with straighter lines and corners.

It is possible to tween more than one letter or number together, but the results are erratic. If you want to shape tween a whole word, do it by putting each letter on a separate layer and creating each tween individually.

4 Select Window> Panels>Frame from the Menu bar to access the Frame panel. Select the Tweening tab and select Shape as the type of tweening.

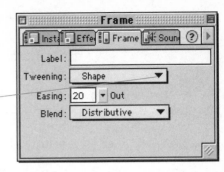

5 Turn on onion skinning to see the path of the shape tween

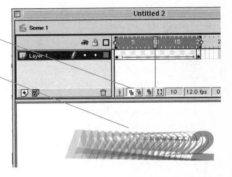

6 It is possible to change the size, colour and orientation of the tweened objects, in their keyframes, by using the drawing tools and their options. This can give added effect. Here, the 2 has been resized and rotated and this is reflected during the tween

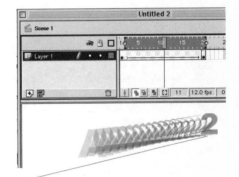

Shape hints

Sometimes the results of a shape tween can be less than ideal; during the course of the tween the object looks more like an ungainly blob rather than one item morphing into another. To improve the tweening process, it is possible to add shape hints to each object. These are corresponding points on each object that act as guides for the tween to follow. To add shape hints to a shape tween:

Up to 26 shape hints can be added to the objects in a shape tween. These are labelled a–z.

Each object in the shape tween has to have the same shape hint applied to it, i.e. if the first object has an 'a' shape hint then the second object has to have the same one.

When a shape hint is added to the first object, the corresponding shape hint will appear when you select the frame containing the second object. It can then be placed by clicking and dragging it.

1 Select the object in frame 1. Select Modify>Transform> Add Shape Hint from the Menu bar

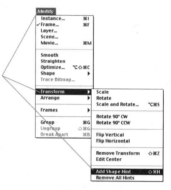

2 Position the shape hint on the object in frame 1

3 Move to the object in frame 20 and position the shape hint in the same corresponding position as for the object in frame 1

4 Continue until a suitable number of shape hints have been added to each object

Animating text

One of the most common uses for Flash on the Web is creating animated text. This is where text moves across the screen from left to right, or vice versa, or fades in and out from a particular point. In some cases, numerous pieces of text are animated within a single movie and, if it is done well, this can create a visually striking effect. To create animated text:

1 Create a text block and convert it into a graphic symbol. Create a motion tween to move it across the screen

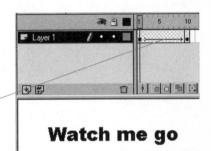

Watch me go

2 Select the text on the Stage in frame 1. Access the Effect panel by selecting Window>Panels> Effect from the Menu bar. Set the Alpha option to 0%. This will make the text fade in as it progresses through the tween

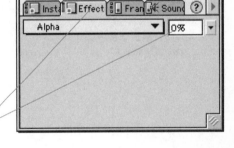

3 Create tweens with text on several layers for added effect. Vary the start and end points of the tweens to achieve variety

Watch me go

I can fade

And me too

Movie clips

Movie clips are symbols that act like self contained animations: they have their own Timeline and once they are created they are placed in the Library. They can then be reused by inserting them anywhere on the main Timeline. This is useful if you have an animation that you want to use several times. To create a movie clip symbol:

Any elements that can be added to an animation in the main editing environment can also be added to a movie clip symbol.

1 Select Insert> New Symbol from the Menu bar. Name the symbol and select Movie Clip

No matter how long a movie clip symbol is (and they can extend over dozens of frames) they are always placed in one frame on the main Timeline.

2 Movie clip Editing Mode looks the same as the main Editing Mode, except that the movie clip icon is shown here. Create the animation as you would for one on the main Stage

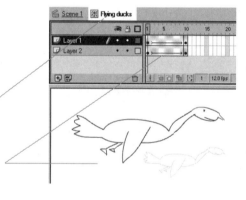

Movie clips can be added to interactive buttons (see Chapter Ten).

3 When the movie clip is completed, click on the scene number to return to the main Editing Mode. The movie clip symbol will be placed in the Library and can be reused throughout the movie

Interactivity

Giving the user the power to interact with a movie is an important part of Flash. This chapter looks at the ways in which this interactivity can be achieved with frames and buttons and also looks at some options for using interactive actions. This includes creating features such as disjointed rollovers and rollover navigation bars, which can be used to great effect on Web pages or in presentations.

Covers

Chapter Ten

Types of interactivity

In addition to its graphical and animated elements, another important aspect of Flash is its interactive functions. These can allow the movie author to instruct the program to perform certain actions when it reaches a certain frame, or an action can be performed when the user clicks on a particular button. Also, interactivity can be achieved with text fields, where an action is performed as a result of the user entering text in an editable text box.

Text fields are one of the more complex types of interactivity. More information can be obtained about them by selecting Help>Flash Help Topics from the Menu bar, then selecting Using Type>Creating text fields and editable text, in the Context Help.

For interactivity to occur in a movie there need to be certain elements present:

- An event, which is something that sets the action in progress. This can be a movie reaching a particular frame or the user clicking a button

- An action, which is performed when the event occurs

- A target, which is the item upon which the action is performed

Actions can be inserted into frames or button symbols. If it is a frame action it can be inserted in the layer where the interactivity is to take place, or it can be placed on a separate layer. In a button symbol the action can be placed in one of the states of the button i.e. when the cursor is moved over it, when it is clicked on or when the mouse button is released.

If an action is inserted on a separate layer, the action will apply to all of the frames at that point in the movie, regardless of how many layers there are.

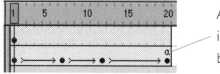

A frame with an action inserted. This is denoted by the small 'a'

Creating interactivity with actions can be a complex business, using some elements of computer programming, the finer points of which could take a whole book themselves. This chapter gives an overview of interactivity and shows some of the commands that can be used.

Frame actions

Actions can only be inserted into keyframes. If they are inserted into regular frames, they will be placed in the nearest preceding keyframe.

Frame actions are placed in a frame and when the Timeline reaches this frame the action passes on an instruction. This could be to stop a movie playing at that point, turn off any sound that is playing or jump to another frame within the movie.

Adding frame actions

The Frame Properties dialog box can also be accessed by selecting a frame and selecting Modify>Frame from the Menu bar.

1   Click once on the frame where you want to add the action. Select Window>Actions to access the Frame Actions panel

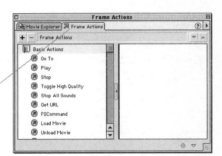

Actions can also be added to objects such as buttons and movie clips (see pages 160–161)

The actions here are displayed with the Actions panel in Normal mode. However, for more advanced programming of actions there is also an Expert mode (see page 168).

2   Double-click on one of the Basic Actions to have it added to the movie. It will then appear in the Actions panel

Numerous different actions can be added to the same frame. When multiple actions are included, they occur in the order in which they were placed.

3   Click here on the down arrow to view and specify the parameters for the selected action

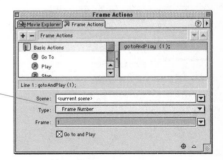

Types of basic actions

The basic actions that can be inserted into a frame are:

- *Go To*. This instructs the movie to jump to the specified frame

- *Play*. This instructs a movie to begin playing

- *Stop*. This stops the movie playing at the specified point. It can be restarted using the Play action

- *Toggle High Quality*. This displays graphics at a higher or lower quality. Also referred to as antialiasing

In addition to the basic actions, there are numerous more advanced ones, for people who have a degree of programming knowledge. The language used in Flash programming is called ActionScript and in Flash 5 it shares the same syntax as JavaScript.

- *Stop All Sounds*. This turns off any sounds that are playing at this point in the movie

- *Get URL*. This instructs the movie to open the specified URL i.e. Web page

- *FS Command*. This lets your movie communicate with the program that is hosting it i.e. a Web browser

- *Load/Unload Movie*. This loads, or unloads, a movie into a Web page

Some frame actions – such as Stop, Play, Toggle High Quality, Stop All Sounds and Go To – are reasonably straightforward. Others – such as FS Command, Set Property and Set Variables – require a certain amount of programming knowledge.

- *Tell Target*. This can be used to interact with other Flash movies by using actions within the current one

- *If Frame is Loaded*. This instructs the movie to perform an action if a certain frame has already been downloaded

- *OnMouseEvent*. This defines a mouse event that has to take place for an action to occur. This is used mainly with object actions, such as for buttons and movie clips

For a fuller look at frame actions select Help>Flash Help Topics from the Menu bar and select Creating Interactive Movies.

More actions

The other categories of actions are:

- Actions

- Operators

- Functions

- Properties

- Objects

These are located underneath the Basic Actions in the Frame Actions panel. Double-click on a category to see the various actions that are available.

Deleting actions

Any action can be deleted from within the Actions dialog box:

When an action is deleted there is no warning box asking if you are sure you want to delete the action. This may not be a problem if it is a simple action such as a 'Stop' one. However, if it is a more complicated action, with several parameters, it could take longer to regenerate it. Make sure you really want to delete an action before you do so.

Click here to change the order of the actions by moving them up or down

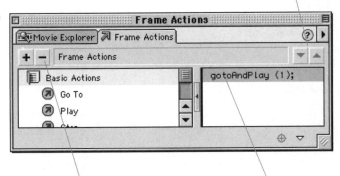

2 Click here to delete the action

1 Access the Frame Actions panel and select an action in the Actions panel

Adding Stop and Play actions

Two of the most commonly used actions are Stop and Play. These do exactly as they say and they can be used at the beginning of a movie or at any point throughout it. The Stop action halts the whole movie at the point where the action is inserted. To restart the movie a Play action has to be activated after the Stop action. Stop actions can be used to stop an animation playing continuously (see page 136). To add Stop and Play actions:

By default, a Flash movie on the Web plays automatically once it is loaded. If you want to pause it at the start, add a Stop action in frame 1 of the movie. This could be used if you want the movie to begin only after the user has performed an action, such as clicking on a button.

If a movie is being used as a stand-alone application, the default is to pause it. To make it play automatically, a Play action (or a Go To and Play action) would have to be inserted in frame 1.

1 Select the frame where you want the movie to stop

2 Access the Frames Action panel by selecting Window>Actions from the Menu bar

Actions can also be added to the Actions panel by dragging and dropping them from the Toolbox list (left panel).

3 Double-click on the Stop action to place it in the Actions Panel

4 Add any other actions you want to include after the Stop action and add Play to restart the movie

Adding Go To actions

Unless instructed otherwise a movie will play all of its frames sequentially. However, by using actions it is possible to change the order in which the frames are played. This could be used if your movie was an interactive game. In one frame could be a question, and the movie would then move to different frames depending on the answer given. To do this you have to insert values for each Go To action. To insert a Go To action:

The Go To action can be used to great effect when it is inserted into a button. See later in this chapter for information about interactive buttons.

The Go To action can be used to jump to any frame in any scene in the movie.

Labels can be used to identify frames as the destination for Go To action, rather than just the frame number.

| Select a frame where you want a Go To action and access the Frame Actions panel as shown on the facing page. Double-click on the Go To action

2 The Go To action is added in the Actions dialog box. By default it goes to the first frame of the current scene. This can be changed if required

3 Select a different scene by clicking here and choosing one from the drop-down list. Enter a different frame number by adding a value here

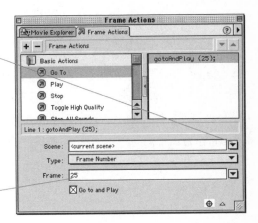

If the target frame for a Go To action is the previous one then there is a danger of inserting an unwanted loop in the movie. If the movie goes back to the previous frame, plays its content and then moves onto the next frame, the Go To action will send it back again, and so on. Another action would have to be inserted in the target frame to avoid it going straight to the next sequential frame (unless a loop effect was intended).

4 Select a target frame for the Go To action by clicking on here and selecting an

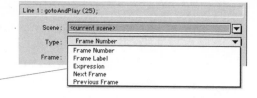

option. This can be a frame number, a label, an expression (a formula based on variable information) or the next or previous frame

5 By default, the Go To action also inserts a Play action. If you want the movie to stop when it reaches the target frame check off the Go to and Play box

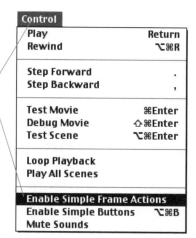

6 Select Control> Enable Simple Frame Actions from the Menu bar to allow you to see how frame actions operate, while you are still in Editing Mode

By default, the Enable Simple Frame Actions option is checked off. This is because it can be irritating for the frame actions to be active when you are editing a movie.

Inserting a preloader

If you have created a long movie, it may take a few seconds for it to download and start playing. This could lead to the user concluding that, since nothing is happening, they should move on somewhere else. To overcome this problem it is possible to create a preloader. This is a message or small animation that assures the user that the movie is loading and will appear shortly. To create a preloader:

Make sure the preloader scene comes before the main movie one.

Since Flash movies use streaming, only part of a movie has to be downloaded before it starts playing. Therefore, when specifying a frame that has to be loaded it does not have to be the last one in the movie. It just has to be enough of the movie to allow it to play while the rest is downloading.

To make sure you specify the correct frame for If Frame is Loaded, check in the Testing environment to see how many frames it takes to preload the main movie. Enter this as the target frame in Step 2 here. For more on testing movies see Chapter Eleven.

1 Create a new movie by selecting File>New from the Menu bar. Create a minimum of two scenes, one for the preloader and one for the main part of the movie. Name Scene 2 Main Movie and create your movie. Name Scene I Preloader and enter suitable content on the Stage

2 Insert a new layer and call this Preload Actions. Select frame I. In the Frame Actions panel, select If Frame is Loaded and specify a frame in the Main Movie scene. This specifies the target frame that has to be loaded before the next action takes effect

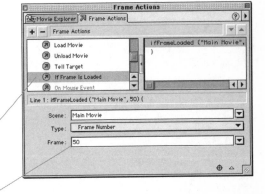

The preloader will keep playing until the criteria in the If Frame Is Loaded action are met. If this takes a reasonable amount of time (over 30 seconds) then it is worth creating a preloader scene that can hold the user's attention.

If a movie is short or small in file size, the preloader may be redundant because the target frame for loading will be in place even before the preloader can be displayed.

When adding the Go To action, make sure the Go to and Play box is checked on.

When testing a preloader, check on the Show Streaming option in the testing environment. For more details on streaming, see Chapter Eleven, page 174.

3 Enter a Go To and Play action underneath the If Frame Is Loaded action. This is the action that will be performed if the criteria for the first action

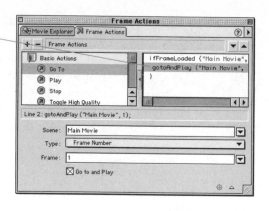

are met i.e. frame 1 of Main Movie will start playing if frame 50 has already been loaded. If it is not met it will move to the next frame

4 Insert a keyframe in frame 2 of the preloader scene and select it. In the Frame Actions panel, enter a Go To and Play action and

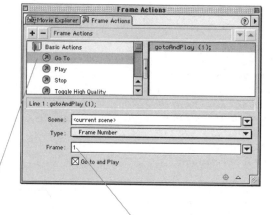

set the parameters as current scene, frame 1. This will send the Timeline back to frame 1 of the preloader scene. It will then check the actions here. If the criteria have not been met it will go to frame 2 again and so on. Once the criteria in frame 1 are met the Timeline will go to the Main Movie scene and begin playing at the specified frame

Button symbols

Creating button symbols

As well as inserting actions into frames in a movie, interactive actions can also be used in buttons. These are a type of symbol that react in certain ways when they are clicked by the user or even when the mouse cursor passes over them. Button symbols can be used in the same way as other symbols: they are created in symbol Editing Mode which then places them in the Library. They can then be dragged onto the Stage, where they become instances of the original button symbol. When a button is created it has four elements, or states:

Using different coloured gradient fills for each state of a button symbol can produce a satisfying effect, where the button appears to glow.

- *Up*. This is how the button appears initially on the Stage, before it has been accessed

- *Over*. This is how the button appears when the mouse cursor is passed over it

- *Down*. This is how the button appears when it is clicked on by the user

- *Hit*. This is the area around the button that is active i.e. if it is clicked it activates the appropriate state. The hit state is invisible in the published movie

Button symbols always have four frames and they act like mini movie clips.

To create a button symbol:

1. Select Insert>New Symbol from the Menu bar

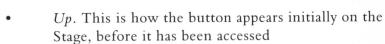

2. In the Symbol Properties dialog name the button and select Button as its behaviour. Click OK

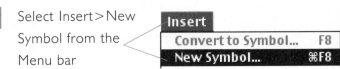

...cont'd

It is possible to tell when you are in button symbol Editing Mode because the button symbol and its name are highlighted at the top of the Timeline, next to the scene name. Also, the four frames have the names of the corresponding button states above them i.e. Up, Over, Down and Hit.

3 Symbol Editing Mode for a button symbol is activated. This is automatically created with four frames, with a keyframe pre-inserted in the first one. The crosshair on the Stage denotes the centre of the button. Draw a circle around the crosshair

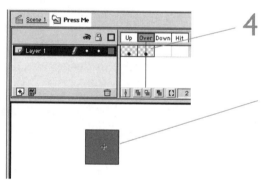

Insert a blank keyframe by selecting Insert> Blank Keyframe from the Menu bar.

4 Select the Over frame and insert a blank keyframe. Draw a square around the crosshair

If you only want to make small changes to an object in a preceding keyframe, such as changing the colour, use the Insert>Keyframe command.

5 Select the Down frame and insert a blank keyframe. Draw a triangle around the crosshair

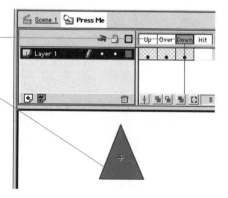

...cont'd

You can make the area defined for the Hit state any colour you like, since it does not appear in the published movie. However, it is a good idea to make it a different colour from the first three states of the button. This way you will know what is the Hit state when you are in symbol Editing Mode.

6 Select the Hit frame and insert a blank keyframe. Draw an object around the crosshair that is large enough to cover the biggest object in the button. This is the area that will activate the button

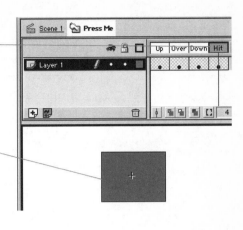

7 Click on the scene name to return to the main Editing Mode. The button symbol will have been placed in the Library. Select the button and click and drag to create an instance on the Stage

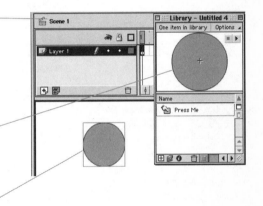

If the Library is not visible, select Window> Library from the Menu bar.

If you try to edit a button instance while Enable Simple Buttons is active, you will only see the different states of the button. Deselect this to perform editing tasks on the Stage.

8 Select Control>Enable Simple Buttons from the Menu bar. This enables you to see how the button performs in its different states, without having to leave the main Editing Mode. The button can also be tested by selecting Control>Test Movie (or Test Scene)

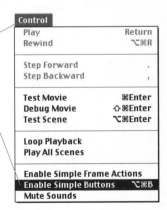

Adding actions to buttons

The same actions that are used for frames can also be used for objects such as buttons and movie clips. However, they are triggered in slightly different ways: button actions are triggered by mouse events i.e. an action performed by the mouse and movie clips are triggered by clip events, which can either be actions by the mouse or a function performed by the movie clip itself. For both types of object the actions that can be added are the same. To add an action to a button:

Button actions should be added to the instance on the Stage rather than the symbol in the Library.

Button actions can be added to the button without first selecting an OnMouseEvent. In this case the default mouse event of Release is added.

Place an instance of a button on the Stage and select it. Access the Object Actions selecting Window> Actions from the Menu bar

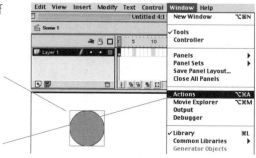

2 In the Object Actions panel select On Mouse Event by double-clicking on it

3 Select a mouse event that will activate the action

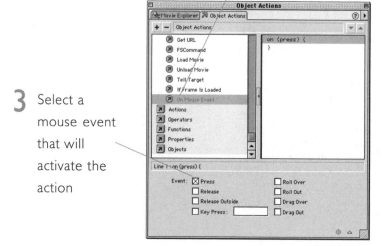

A movie clip can have the same actions added to it as a button. However, these are triggered by OnClipEvents, rather than OnMouseEvents. The OnClipEvents for a movie clip are:

• Load, when the movie clip is loaded into the movie

• Enter frame, when the timeline reaches the frame in which the movie clip is placed

• Unload, which occurs when the movie clip has finished playing

• Mouse down, when the mouse is pressed

• Mouse up, when the mouse is released

• Mouse move, when the mouse is moved over the movie clip

• Key down, when a specific key is pressed

• Key up, when a specific key is released

• Data, when specific information is entered

More than one mouse event can be added to a single button.

The possible mouse event options for buttons are:

• *Press*, which occurs when the mouse button is pressed while the cursor is within the Hit area of a button

• *Release*, which occurs when the mouse button is released within the Hit area

• *Release Outside*, which occurs when the mouse button is released when the cursor has been dragged outside the Hit area

• *Roll Over*, which occurs when the mouse cursor moves into the Hit area

• *Roll Out*, which occurs when the mouse cursor is moved out of the Hit area

• *Drag Over*, which occurs when the mouse button is held down and dragged out of the Hit area and then back into it

• *Drag Out*, which occurs when the mouse button is clicked within the Hit area and then dragged outside it

• *Key Press*, which can be used to specify a key on the keyboard to trigger the action

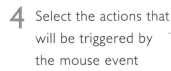 Select the actions that will be triggered by the mouse event

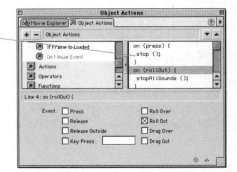

Adding movie clips and sounds

Fully animated buttons can be created by using different movie clips for each state of the button. This means the animation will change in appearance, according to how the user is interacting with the button.

Movie clips

To make buttons more versatile it is possible to add movie clips to them. This means that when the button is pressed (or whatever mouse event that has been assigned to it) a movie clip plays. Movie clips can be inserted in the separate states of a button and different ones can be used within the same button. To add a movie clip to a button:

1 Double-click on a button symbol in the Library to access symbol Editing Mode

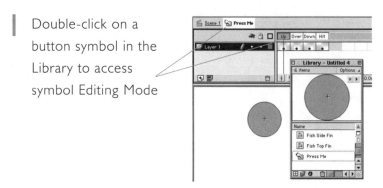

If you are using only movie clips to create a button, make sure that the Hit area of the button is big enough to cover the area of the largest movie clip.

2 Select a state of the button (Up, Over or Down) and drag a movie clip over the button centrepoint. The clip will play when this state of the button is activated

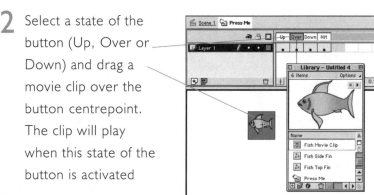

To learn more about adding sounds to a movie, select Help>Flash Help Topics from the Menu bar and then select Adding sound from the Context Help.

Sounds

Sound files can be added to buttons in the same way as movie clips: open the button in symbol Editing Mode, select the Up, Over or Down state and drag a sound file from the Library onto the Stage. This can be a useful technique to alert the user to whether they have performed a particular action with the button i.e. one sound for when they press the button and another for when they release it. Different sounds can be added to the first three states of a button.

Creating disjointed rollovers

When a basic button is created it is often in the form of a simple rollover i.e. when the cursor moves over the button it changes in appearance. This is an effective technique for buttons on Web sites, as a subtle change of colour or text can have a significant impact on the user. However, buttons are a lot more versatile than this and they can also be used to create disjointed rollovers. This is when the rollover (Over) portion of the button appears in a different place to the button itself. To create a disjointed rollover:

It is best to keep the content for the Down state the same as for the Over state. Otherwise the effect can become overdone, with too much happening at once.

1 Create a new button and enter content for the Up state

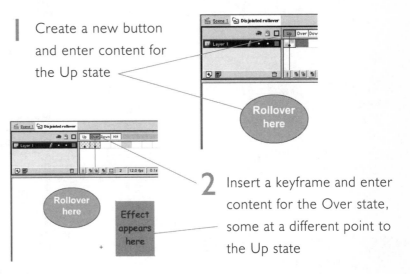

2 Insert a keyframe and enter content for the Over state, some at a different point to the Up state

When adding the Hit area for a disjointed rollover button, make sure that it only covers the same area as the content in the Up state, not the Over or Down states. Otherwise, the effect will be activated at the wrong time i.e. when you rollover the area of the Over state rather than just the Up state.

3 Enter content for the Down and Hit states. For the Down state this can be the same as the Over state or different. When the button is activated it appears like this

4 When the button is rolled over, the content for the Over state appears. This is the disjointed effect

Adding invisible buttons

On some occasions it is useful to have invisible buttons in a Flash movie. These are buttons that have no visible content in either the Up, Over or Down state, but they do have a hit area. Object actions can then be added to the button so that the user can interact with the movie without knowing it. One use for invisible buttons is in the creation of rollover navigation bars (see the next page). To create an invisible button:

Invisible buttons can be placed behind text, to give the user the impression that the action is connected with the text block when in fact it is part of the button.

When an instance of an invisible button is created on the Stage, the Hit area is visible, so that you know the exact location of the button.

The Object Actions panel is accessed by clicking once on the button instance on the Stage and selecting Window>Actions from the Menu bar.

1 Create a new symbol and give it a Button behaviour and a recognisable name

2 Insert a keyframe into the Up state of the button, but do not put any content on the Stage. Repeat this for the Over and Down states but enter content for the Hit state

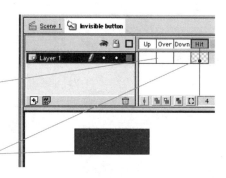

3 Drag an instance of the invisible button onto the Stage. Access the Object Actions panel and add any required actions to the button

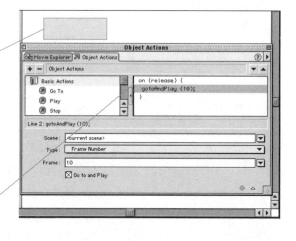

Creating rollover navigation bars

Rollover navigation bars are an increasingly popular way for Web designers to provide a means of navigation around sites. They are a set of buttons that, when a mouse event occurs, reveal submenus for that particular topic. The user can then click on the submenu, or, if they roll away from the submenu button, they are taken back to the start of the menu. This is achieved with a mixture of visible and invisible buttons and the corresponding button actions. These can be written in JavaScript, but it also possible to create them in Flash (for which no programming knowledge is required):

Before you start creating a rollover navigation bar, sketch it out on a piece of paper first. This way you will have a clear understanding of what is required in each frame.

The reason for putting a Stop action in frame 1 is to ensure that this frame remains visible when the movie is opened, rather than it starting to play through the rest of the frames.

Be careful if you are using a Flash rollover navigation bar if you are using a Web site that contains frames and framesets. This is because it can cause real confusion when targeting the links in the navigation bar.

1 Create a button symbol and place an instance of it on the Stage in frame I of the movie

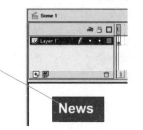

2 Double-click on frame I and enter a Stop action from the Frame Actions panel

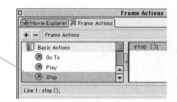

3 Select the button instance by clicking on it once and access the Object Action panel. Select Release for the OnMouseEvent and then select the Go To and Stop action. Enter Frame 2 as the target frame for the action

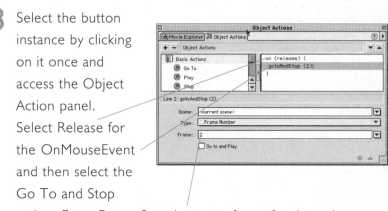

4 Insert a keyframe in frame 2 and insert the content for the submenu. This can consist of drawing objects and text. They do not need to be created as buttons because all of the functionality will be added with invisible buttons.

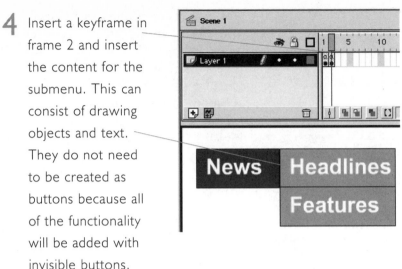

Add a stop action into the frame that contains this content. This will ensure that the movie stops at this point and so allows the menu to be displayed

5 Create an invisible button, which is exactly the same size as the area for each submenu. Place an invisible button over each submenu area, so that it covers it completely

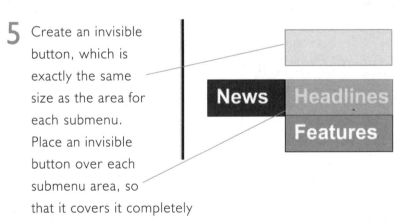

...cont'd

In the example on the right the invisible button will keep the user on the existing frame, i.e. the submenus, when they rollover the invisible button. If they roll away from it, in any direction, they will be taken to frame 1. However, if they press and release the button, the Get URL action will be activated.

Using this technique, complex rollover navigation bars can be created. Add more buttons to the main menu in frame 1 and then create the submenus for each item in subsequent frames, i.e. 2, 3, 4 etc. Add the appropriate actions to all of the buttons in the main menu, so that they go to the correct frame for the corresponding submenu.

In all of the subsequent frames, add stop actions and also the invisible button that takes the movie back to the main menu (i.e. frame 1) if one of the submenu options is not selected.

Select View>Rulers from the Menu bar to get a better idea of the dimensions of the navigation bar.

6 Give each instance of the invisible button the same set of Object Actions:

- OnMouseEvent: Rollover
- Go To and Stop, frame 2;
- OnMouseEvent: Rollout
- Go To and Stop, frame 1;
- OnMouseEvent: Release
- Get URL, (enter required URL)

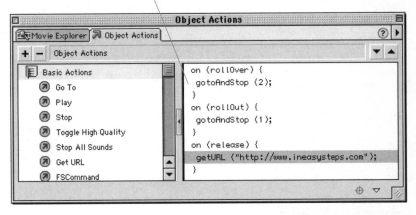

7 When the rollover navigation bar is completed, select Movie>Movie from the Menu bar and enter

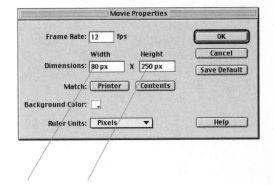

dimensions for the width and height of the movie to match the size of the navigation bar. This way, when the movie is inserted into a Web page there will not be wasted space around it.

Expert Mode and ActionScript

Using Expert Mode

If you are not experienced in using ActionScript then creating actions in Normal Mode will probably suit your purposes more than adequately. However, if you do know some ActionScript then you may find this a useful option. Also, if you can program in JavaScript then you will find this familiar because in Flash 5 the two languages now share the same programming syntax.

Expert mode allows you to write you own ActionScript code in the Action List, or edit existing code. You can add actions from the Toolkit on the left of the actions panel, but there are no Basic actions available (it is presumed that if you know some ActionScript, then you will be able to create the coding for these yourself). Also, there are no parameters available for actions in Expert Modes, these too have to be entered manually. To access Expert Mode:

If you want Expert Mode to appear as the default whenever the Object or Frame action panels are displayed, select Edit>Preferences from the Menu bar. Select the General tab and under Actions Panel select Mode: Expert Mode.

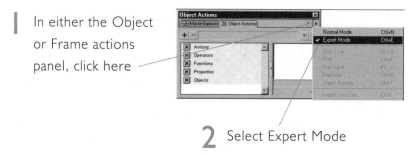

I In either the Object or Frame actions panel, click here

2 Select Expert Mode

It is possible to instruct Flash to check the ActionScript in a movie and display any problems with the coding. This is known as debugging and it can be done in the authoring environment by selecting Control>Debug Movie or in the Testing environment by selecting Window>Debugger. Further information about debugging can be found in the ActionScript Reference within the Flash Help pages (see the facing page).

3 The available action groups are displayed here

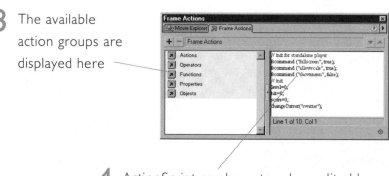

4 ActionScript can be entered or edited here

Using ActionScript

In Flash 5 the actual ActionScript code is displayed in the Actions panel when an action is selected.

ActionScript is an object-orientated computer programming language that shares considerable similarities with JavaScript, including the coding syntax. It is used to add the elements of interactivity into a Flash movie and, if used to its full potential, it is an extremely powerful tool. However, this also means that it is not something that can be picked up in a few days. If you have experience of other programming languages then it will be easier to get to grips with ActionScript, but if you want to learn it from scratch, it will probably take several months to become proficient. If you want to learn about ActionScript, or you have some knowledge of it and would like to learn more, there are various sites available within Flash Help:

You do not have to have any knowledge of ActionScript to produce effective, and interactive, movies in Flash. If you use the Actions panel in Normal Mode then all of the necessary script is inserted for you and all you have to worry about is inserting the right commands, with the relevant parameters.

1 Select Help> ActionScript Reference from the Menu bar to access the Help section with general information about ActionScript

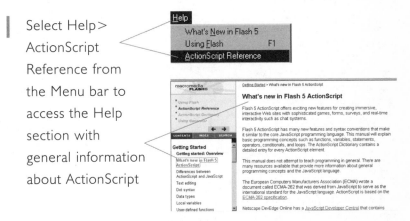

When you insert actions with either the Frame Actions or the Object Actions panels it is worth having a look at the ActionScript code that is created, so that you can become familiar with its appearance.

2 Select Help> ActionScript Dictionary from the Menu bar to access the Help section with details of every ActionScript element

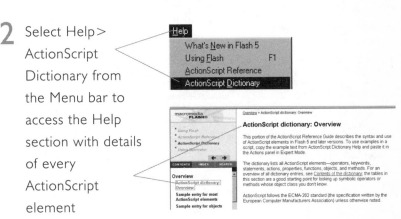

Movie Explorer

When a movie is being created, it is easy to lose track of all of the elements that have been added. In addition to drawing objects, texts and instances, there are also all of the actions and it can be confusing remembering where all of these are and what they do. To simplify matters in this respect, Flash 5 has a new innovation in the form of the Movie Explorer. This displays a graphical and hierarchical layout of all the elements within the movie. To access the Movie Explorer:

As well as providing a graphical and hierarchical display of the contents of a movie, the Movie Explorer can also perform a number of editing and organisational tasks. This is done through the Options menu, which can be access by clicking on the right-pointing arrow in the top right corner of the Movie Explorer panel:

Some of the tasks that can be performed through the options menu are:

- Searching for an named element;
- Searching for all occurrences of a symbol instance;
- Search for words, or fonts;
- Copy text so that it can be used in an external spell checker.

1 Select Window> Movie Explorer from the Menu bar

2 Click here to display text, symbols, actions, multimedia

3 Click here to display frames and layers, and display settings

4 Click on a right pointing arrow (Mac) or + sign (Windows) to display the contents of a particular element i.e. the actions for a symbol

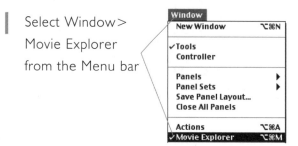

Testing and publishing

The final part of producing a Flash movie is testing it to ensure it works properly and then publishing it for people to see. This chapter looks at ways to test the elements of a movie, set publishing options and then publish a movie, either on the Web or as a stand-alone application.

Covers

Chapter Eleven

Testing options

The Controller is a quick way to test animations without having to leave the authoring environment. Another way is to drag the Playhead along the Timeline, although this may not play it at a consistent speed.

As with any project that is going to be viewed by a large audience, it is important to test movies thoroughly before they are published. Within a Flash movie there can be a number of complex elements and it is essential to make sure that everything is working properly, both independently and as part of the whole movie. Flash has several testing options and the ones in the authoring environment are:

The Controller

This plays a movie through in the authoring environment. It shows animations but buttons and frame actions are inactive. To use the Controller:

1   Select Window>
    Toolbars>Controller
    from the Menu bar
    (Windows) or
    Window>Controller
    (Mac)

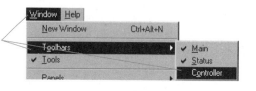

The Controller can be moved around the screen by clicking the top bar and dragging.

2   Use the controls to play the movie:

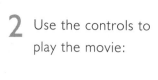

Rewind   Play   Go to end

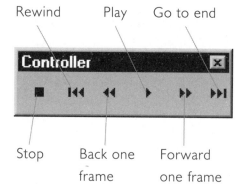

Stop   Back one frame   Forward one frame

The Enable Frame Actions and Enable Buttons options should only be used when you want to test these items. Otherwise they could interfere with other editing processes.

Enable buttons and frames

Frame actions and buttons can be viewed in the authoring environment:

1   Select Control>Enable Simple Frame Actions (or Control>Enable Simple Buttons) in the Menu bar

When it is first accessed, the testing environment will look similar to the authoring one. The only difference is that most of the Menu bar and toolbar options are greyed out. However, there are a number of features that can be accessed in the testing environment that allow greater versatility when testing a movie. These are looked at on the following pages.

Rather than just testing individual parts of a movie, as with the options in the authoring environment on the facing page, it is also possible to test an entire scene or movie to see how it will appear when it is published:

Testing scenes

To test an individual scene:

1 Open the scene you want to test and select Control>Test Scene from the Menu bar

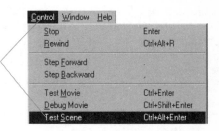

2 This will open the selected scene and play it in the testing environment. Animations, frame actions and buttons will all be active

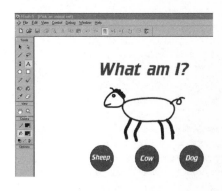

To return to the authoring environment from the testing one, close down the testing window or select File>Close from the Menu bar.

Testing movies

This performs a very similar task to Test Scene, except that it tests all of the scenes in a movie, in the order in which they will play when the movie is published. To test a movie:

Select Control>Test Movie from the Menu bar

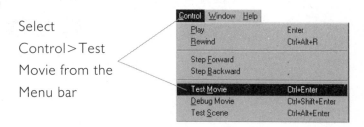

Testing environment

When a Flash movie is played over a browser on the Web it is impossible to predict how it will appear on every user's computer. This is because of the wide range of browsers being used, processor speeds and modem speeds: on one computer the movie may play perfectly, but on another it may take longer to download and play erratically. Flash has a number of functions to test how a movie will play in different circumstances.

Test movies at the lowest download speed first (14.4K). If they work well at this speed then there should be no problem at the higher speeds. However, test them at the higher ones too, just to make sure.

Testing download speeds

Due to the diversity of modems used by people when accessing the Internet it is certain that your movie will be downloaded at a variety of speeds. You can test how various options will look by using the streaming option in the testing environment:

The User Settings and the Customize option for download speeds can be used for settings outside the most commonly used ones which are 14K, 28K and 56K. The custom settings can be used for high speed connections or if the movie is being used on an intranet. If this is the case, check the required setting with your system administrator.

1 In the testing environment for a scene or a movie, select Debug from the Menu bar and select the required download speed

2 Select View > Show Streaming to see how your movie will play at the selected download speed

Bandwidth Profiler

A Bandwidth Profiler is available in the testing environment and this can display several items of useful information about the streaming of the movie and how individual frames affect this. To view the Bandwidth Profiler:

Streaming is a technique which allows a movie to start playing when only part of the whole movie has been downloaded. If this works properly the movie should play smoothly throughout.

However, problems can occur if there are very large frames in a movie since the movie will already be playing and the downloading will be slowed down. If the playback of the movie catches up with the streaming download then there could be a pause in the playing of the movie.

1   In the testing environment select View>Bandwidth Profiler from the Menu bar

View	Control	Debug	Window	Help
Zoom In			Ctrl+=	
Zoom Out			Ctrl+-	
Magnification				▶
Bandwidth Profiler			Ctrl+B	

2   The Bandwidth Profiler is displayed above the movie

Movie:
Dim: 726 X 260 pixels
Fr Rate: 15.0 fr/sec
Size: 37 KB (38824 B)
Duration: 202 fr (13.5 s)
Preload: 307 fr (20.5 s)
Settings:
Bandwidth: 1200 B/s (80 B/fr)
State:
Frame: 78
0 KB (31 B)
Loaded: 100.0 % (202 frames)
37 KB (38826 B)

The elements of the Bandwidth Profiler are:

• *Dim*. This is the dimensions of your movie, in pixels

• *Fr Rate*. This is the Frames Per Second speed at which your movie is set to play

• *Size*. This is the file size of the entire movie or scene

• *Duration*. This is the total number of frames in the movie (or scene). The number beside it, in brackets, is the time the movie (or scene) will take to play, in seconds

- *Preload*. This is the time the movie will take to download before it starts to play. This information is particularly relevant if you want to include a preloader with a movie (see Chapter Ten)

- *Bandwidth*. This is the bandwidth speed that has been selected to test the download speed of the movie

- *Frame*. The first number is where the Playhead is currently situated and the one underneath it displays a selected frame's size in relation to the whole movie

- *Loaded*. The first number displays how many frames of the movie have been downloaded and the one underneath displays the amount of the file that has been downloaded

To maximise streaming, try to use symbols frequently in a movie and bitmaps and sounds sparingly.

With the Bandwidth Profiler showing, Select View>Show Streaming to view how the movie will download. A green line moves along the Timeline to indicate how much of the movie has been downloaded in the background. The cursor indicates where the movie's Playhead is currently positioned. If the two meet and stop, this could indicate a problem area in the downloading of a movie.

Streaming Graph

When used in conjunction with the Bandwidth Profiler the Streaming Graph can identify potential problem areas for when a movie is downloading. To access the Streaming Graph:

1 In the testing environment, select View>Streaming Graph

2 Bars above this (red) line indicate frames that could cause a problem when downloading

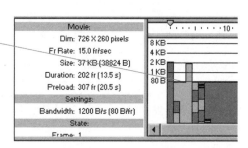

Frame-ßy-Frame graph

Another option for assessing the downloading speed of a
movie is the Frame-By-Frame graph. This shows the size of
each frame in a movie. To view the Frame-By-Frame graph:

*If a few frames
stand out as
being a lot
bigger in size
than the others
in the movie, return to the
authoring environment and
see if they can be edited.*

1 In the testing
environment, select
View>Frame-By-
Frame Graph

*On the View
menu select
Quality and
click on either
Low, Medium
or High to see the movie at
a higher or lower quality.*

2 The size of each individual frame in the movie is displayed in
the graph. Select an individual frame to view its properties in
the Bandwidth Profiler

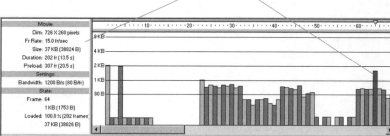

Preparing to publish

The object of creating any Flash movie is to have it published. This can be onto a CD-ROM as a stand-alone application, but the most common use for Flash movies is to publish them on the Web or an intranet.

The method for publishing Flash movies on the Web is to insert them into an HTML document. If you look at the code for a file on the Web containing a Flash movie you may want to run screaming from your computer, never to think of Flash or HTML again. At first sight it does look confusing, even if you have some experience of producing Web pages. The good news is that you only have to specify a few settings and Flash does all of the complicated work for you. This is done by instructing Flash to create an HTML document with the Flash movie inserted in it. However, before this, certain settings can be chosen to determine the way the movie will look when it is published.

If you select HTML as a format for publishing your movie, the Flash option is selected automatically, if it is not already.

Publish settings for the Web

To determine the settings for a movie on the Web:

Flash can create files in several formats and it is possible to give each file type a different name. However, for the sake of consistency it is better to keep the same root name for all formats (the extension will be different for each type). The default uses the same name for each format.

1 In the authoring environment, select File > Publish Settings

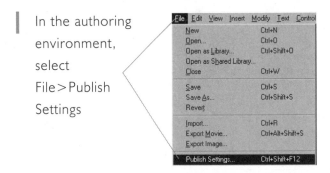

A new publishing addition in Flash 5 is the option for publishing Flash movies in a format that can be viewed on a RealPlayer.

2 Select Flash and HTML as the type. This will create a Flash movie file (Shockwave Flash or .SWF) and an HTML file (.HTM)

If you click on the Info button next to the Template box there will be a description of the template and any HTML tags it uses.

3 In the Publish Settings dialog box select the HTML tab

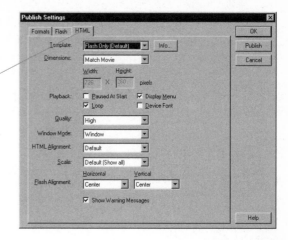

HTML settings

Within the HTML dialog box there are various settings to determine the appearance of the Flash movie in your HTML document:

The options for specifying the dimensions of a published movie do not affect its positioning within the HTML window, just its location in the movie window.

- *Template*. This is how the movie is inserted into the HTML document. The simplest one is the default, Flash Only, which uses EMBED and OBJECT tags to display the movie depending on which browser it is being viewed on (EMBED for Netscape Navigator or Communicator and OBJECT for Internet Explorer). The other available templates are: Flash with FS Command; Image Map; Java Player; QuickTime; and User Choice. These can be used to give extra functionality to a movie, but if you are not confident with these then the default is more than adequate

- *Dimensions*. This dictates how the movie will appear within a movie window within the HTML document window. The default is to match the size set in the Movie Properties dialog box. However, the size can also be set in pixels or as a percentage to make the movie larger or smaller than the movie window, as appropriate

In order to get the correct position for your published movie, experiment with the Dimensions, Scale and Flash Alignment settings to see how different combinations appear in a browser.

There is also an option for Window Mode which can be used to create movies with transparent backgrounds (see page 183).

HTML editors can be used to include additional content, as well as the Flash movie.

- *Playback.* The options here determine the properties for when the movie is played in a browser. These are: Paused At Start, which means the movie does not start playing until the user performs an action such as clicking a button; Display Menu, which displays a contextual menu about the Flash Player if the user right-clicks (Windows) or Ctrl+clicks (Mac); Loop, which will cause the movie to keep playing after its initial playback; and Device Font (Windows only), which substitutes suitable fonts if the ones in the movie are not installed on the user's computer

- *Quality.* This can be used to get the best balance between playback speed and image quality. The options range from Low, which is the fastest speed and the lowest image quality, to Best, which offers the top image quality but the slowest playback speed

- *HTML Alignment.* This can be used if you create an HTML page with other items in addition to the Flash movie. This allows you to align the movie with the other items on the page. The options are Left, Right, Top and Bottom

- *Scale.* If you have changed the dimensions of the movie from its original settings this can be used to determine how it is scaled within the movie window. The options are: Show All, which scales the movie proportionately to fit the movie window; No Border, which will display the movie at its actual size even if it is bigger than the movie window; and Exact Fit, which scales the movie to fit exactly into the whole movie window

- *Flash Alignment.* This can be used to determine the movie's position within the movie window. The options are for Horizontal – Left, Center and Right; and for Vertical – Top, Center and Bottom

- *Show Warning Messages.* This alerts the user to any problems with the HTML coding

Flash settings

In addition to determining the HTML settings for a movie, the same can be done for Flash settings.

Select the Flash tab in the Publish Settings dialog box

The Flash settings are:

- *Load Order.* This lets you set the order in which layers within a frame are loaded into the browser

- *Generate size report.* If this is checked on, a text file will be created, reporting on the size of each frame

- *Protect from import.* This stops anyone copying your movie and using it as their own

- *Omit Trace actions.* This stops anyone being able to look at the code that makes up a movie

- *Debugging Permitted.* This can be used with the Password option to allow remote debugging of movies

- *JPEG Quality.* This can be used to set the quality of JPEG images

- *Audio Stream.* This can be used to compress streamed sounds

- *Audio Event.* This can be used to compress event sounds

- *Version.* This can be used so earlier version of the Flash Player can view your movie

More publishing options

Although HTML is the most common way to publish Flash movies there are a number of other options, which can all be accessed by selecting the Formats tab in the Publish Settings dialog box. The other formats are:

Projectors are an excellent way to distribute Flash movies, particularly as the user does not require a Flash Player or any other plug-in to play them.

- *Projectors*. These are stand-alone applications that act like mini programs, that can be played on almost any computer. Everything that is needed to play the movie is contained within the projector file and it is just a case of opening it from a CD-ROM, a floppy disk or a hard drive

- *QuickTime*. This is a video and multimedia file format that has been developed by Apple and it is widely used for playing videos on the Web. The QuickTime format has its own dialog box and a Flash movie can be incorporated with other items in a QuickTime movie. The QuickTime dialog box lets you set the size of the QuickTime movie and how the Flash movie interacts with other elements

To download the QuickTime 4 plug-in visit the following Web site:

- *http://www.apple.com/*

- *Graphic formats*. There are dialog boxes for three different graphic formats: GIFs, JPEGs and PNGs. This allows you to apply a variety of settings to determine how these images are displayed in the published movie

The RealPlayer setting also creates a video format but the movie has to be saved as a version in Flash 4. To do this, select the required version under the Flash settings under Publish Settings.

All file formats for a Flash movie (except Projector) have their own dialog boxes. Click a tab in the Publish Settings dialog to access them

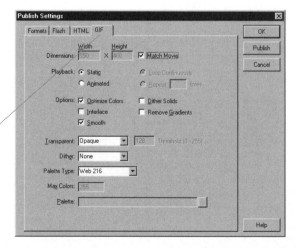

Creating a transparent movie

One of the most effective, and frequently overlooked, uses for Flash is the creation of small movies that can be included as part of an HTML page on the Web, without dominating the rest of the content. This can be particularly useful for company logos and the suchlike. With items like this, it is useful to be able to make the background of the movie transparent, so that when it is placed on a Web page, the background of the HTML page is visible behind the Flash movie. To achieve this:

The default setting for the rulers is pixels. If you want to change this, select Modify>Movie from the Menu bar and select the required unit of measurement from the Ruler>Units box.

1 Create a Flash movie that contains a logo or similar icon. Make sure the rulers are showing by selecting View>Rulers

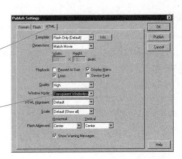

If you do not modify the size of the movie to match the content on the Stage, the transparent effect will still be applied to the whole movie. However, you will have less scope for adding content around it on the HTML page because the movie will take up a greater amount of space and you will not be able to place any content on top of it.

2 Select Modify>Movie from the Menu bar and enter the dimensions of the movie so that the object takes up all of the space on the Stage

3 Select File>Publish Settings from the Menu bar. Select the HTML tab and in the Windows Mode box select Transparent Windowless

For more information on Dreamweaver, see Computer Step's 'Dreamweaver in easy steps' title.

When creating the HTML page for the transparent Flash movie, use the one that was produced during the Publish operation in Flash itself, and then add additional content to it.

It is possible to create an HTML page in a Web authoring program and then insert the transparent Flash movie, but this will result in the transparent effect not working. The command to make the movie transparent is inserted into the HTML document when it is created in Flash.

Flash movies like this can be resized within a Web authoring program in the same way as you would resize a graphical image. Since they are created with vectors they do not lose any definition, regardless of their new size.

4 Publish the movie (see the facing page) so that an HTML file is created. Open this in a Web authoring program such as Dreamweaver

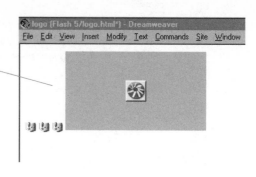

5 Enter a background for the HTML page. The Flash movie icon will appear on top of it

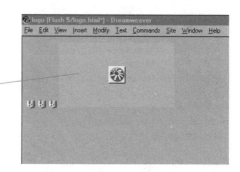

6 Save the HTML page and view it in a browser. The background colour will be visible through the Flash movie. If it is not transparent, it would look like this

Publishing a movie

Once you have chosen the format, or formats, for your movie and assigned the necessary settings it is time to publish your work.

Previewing

Before the movie is actually published it is possible to see exactly what it will look like in each of the chosen formats:

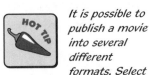

It is possible to publish a movie into several different formats. Select each format in the Publish Settings dialog. When you select Publish, Flash will create the appropriate files for all of these formats.

Select File>Publish Preview from the Menu bar and select the format in which you want to view the movie

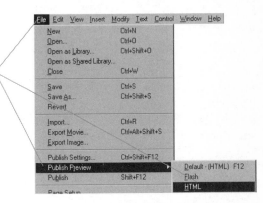

The Projector format creates the largest file size of all Flash formats.

Publishing

If you are satisfied with the preview of your movie you can then publish it:

> Select File>Publish from the Menu bar

Movie file (.SWF) Authoring file (.FLA)

After step 1, Flash creates files for all of the formats that were selected in the Publish Settings dialog and places them in the same folder as the original movie.

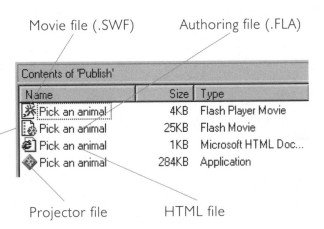

Projector file HTML file

Publishing on the Web

An HTML file is made up of a set of instructions that tell the browser what to display at certain points. Since the Flash movie is referred to in the HTML document it has to be on the server too so that the browser can display it.

If you are publishing a Flash movie on the Web you will need to upload your HTML file and the Flash movie file (.SWF) to the Web server where your site will be hosted. Check with you Internet Service Provider (ISP), or system administrator if you are publishing over an intranet, that they are capable of displaying Flash and ask if there are any specific settings they require.

Once your HTML page is published the source code will look something like this:

Of the two files that are created when a movie is put together, the movie itself has a .SWF extension and the authoring file has a .FLA extension.

(The .SWF file is the one that is uploaded to the Web server.)

This HTML coding is generated by Flash during the Publish process

Using an HTML editor

Flash movies can make up the entire contents of an HTML document. However, if you use an HTML editor (such as Microsoft FrontPage, Adobe Go Live, Adobe PageMill or Macromedia DreamWeaver), it is possible to create additional content on the HTML page. This is an excellent way to combine a Flash movie into a larger HTML document on the Web. There are two important considerations when you are publishing Flash sites on the Web:

If you are including a link on a Web page for downloading the Flash Player, it should go to:

• http://www.macromedia. com/shockwave/ download/

(Omit all spaces in the address.)

- Always include a plain HTML version of your site, for users who do not have the Flash Player installed, or who do not want to download it

- Include a link for those users who want to download the latest version of the Flash Player

Index